AMERINDIANS, CAPUCHINS & CEDULANTS

A Brief History of Couva
From Earliest Times to 1797

Revised Edition

STEVE H. DIXON

authorHOUSE

AuthorHouse™
1663 Liberty Drive
Bloomington, IN 47403
www.authorhouse.com
Phone: 1 (800) 839-8640

Published by AuthorHouse 03/28/2020

ISBN: 978-1-7283-0814-2 (sc)
ISBN: 978-1-7283-0815-9 (hc)
ISBN: 978-1-7283-0813-5 (e)

Library of Congress Control Number: 2019903989

Print information available on the last page.

This book is printed on acid-free paper.

In memory of my parents,
Robert and Hannah Dixon

CONTENTS

ILLUSTRATIONS AND MAPS

PREFACE

Several years ago, I received a copy of a booklet titled *Caroni Limited in Trinidad,* published by Tate and Lyle Limited, a British company. The booklet contained a description of its subsidiary, Caroni Limited. Caroni Limited was a sugar producing company located in Couva, Trinidad, when it was a going concern. The cover of the booklet featured a map of Trinidad, which dated back to the year 1800 and published by Robert Laurie and James Whittle. It was there on the map that I noticed the *Indian Village of Savanette* situated near Couva, my hometown.

I have been intrigued by this village since then and my intrigue eventually became the motivating factor behind my intermittent yet continuing research on its history. Somewhere along the process, I was stimulated to broaden the scope of my research into the early history of Couva. Now, I have put pen to paper to narrate to everyone the fascinating history of the town.

This book offers a brief historic account of early Couva, which can help readers learn how this region transitioned over the years to become what it is today!

This revised edition of my book incorporates new material, including an extract from Father Arcangel de Barcelona's 1687 manuscript titled *Viaje desde el Puerto de Cadiz a la Isla de Trinidad y Recorrido de la Misma* which describes the founding of the third Capuchin mission in Trinidad (i.e., Santa Anna de Savaneta in Couva).

I wish to express my heartfelt appreciation to everyone who has assisted me throughout the course of my research. I especially want to thank Father Valenti Serra de Manresa of the Arxiu Provincial dels Caputxins de Catalunya, Barcelona and Manuel Posso for graciously providing me with a copy of Father Arcangel's diary. Finally, I also express my sincere gratitude to my wife Jennifer for her unwavering support and patience during every step of the way.

Steve Dixon
Couva, Trinidad
31 January 2020

CHAPTER 1

This chapter gives an overview of Couva, its brief history and its early peoples. Early settlers called Couva, "Cuba". Later French settlers came to the island and changed the name of the town as per their own language and dialect. Amerindians, Missionaries, the French planters, along with their Black slaves, and the Spanish colonial policies shaped the history of Couva.

COUVA: AN OVERVIEW

Couva, a town on the island of Trinidad, enjoys a central location on the island's western coast, about 25 miles away (by car) from the capital city of Port of Spain. According to the most recent census, which was conducted in 2011, the total population of greater Couva was approximately 30,000, while central Couva's population was 3,861. However, Couva has since seen a radical increase with the significant influx of a new population.

Couva was originally called "Cuba" by the early settlers. According to Alfred Carrada (2003), a Taino (i.e., Arawak) language lexicographer, the name *Cuba* is derived from the word *cubao*, an Arawakan word meaning *where fertile land is abundant* (The Dictionary of the Taino Language, para. 35). (Some later historical records have also referred to the region as "Cuva", an anglicised Spanish version of the name *Cuba*). Later, after the French Caribbean immigrants arrived in Trinidad and French became the principal language of the island, the name Cuba (or

1

Cuva) was changed to "Couva", and it remains the name of the town to the present day (Laurence, 1975, p. 131).

In 1802, F. Mallet, the captain of the surveying engineers of the British forces in the West Indies, published a map of Trinidad that showed "Rio de Cuba", which is now called the Couva River (See *Map Section 5*). *Rio de Cuba* is a Spanish name that translates to the *River of Cuba* in English, obviously taking its name from the region called Cuba. On the map, the region immediately south of *Rio de Cuba* was called "Savaneta" and the area immediately north of it was called "Cascajal". Hence, wherever Savaneta (sometimes written as *Savenatta, Savanette, Savoneta, Savonetta* and *Sabaneta*) or Cascajal is mentioned in historical literature, it refers to Couva. The word *Savaneta* means *little savannah* or *little plain*, while Cascajal means a *place full of gravel and pebbles*. One of Couva's western regions retains the name *Couva Savannah* until today.

Two significant factors shaped the history of *old* Couva (i.e., Savaneta): the arrival of four distinct groups of peoples—Amerindians, Missionaries, and French planters along with their Black slaves—and Spain's colonial policies.

Couva is a modern, pulsating town that is prosperous and sufficiently well populated. But the town wasn't always as lively and contemporary as it is today. Old Couva had been settled by Amerindians who originated in South America. The indigenes may have lived in an *encomienda* in Savenata, under the rule of a Spanish lord, at one time during their history.

From being a stretch of mostly uncultivated fertile soil, to being the centre of the Saint Anne's Mission, founded by Roman Catholic Capuchin missionaries in Eastern Couva, to convert the "pagan" Amerindians to Christianity as part of Spain's colonial policy, it emerged, after the closure of the mission, as primarily sugar plantation estates functioning profitably off the brutal exploitation of Black slaves as labourers.

Spanish policy encouraged Catholic foreigners, mostly the French settlers from other West Indian islands, to migrate to Trinidad along with their Black slaves, capital, and entrepreneurial spirit to develop the island's economy and to increase its population. To lure foreigners to the island, the King of Spain issued the *Cedula of Population* (1783), which offered generous land grants and other incentives. Couva was one area where the Spanish government granted land to these immigrant planters to grow crops. Due to its fertile soils, the planters mostly cultivated sugarcane.

Couva sprang up as a new community called Exchange Village— quite different from the Catholic mission— around St. Paul's Roman Catholic Church post-emancipation until today when it has become Trinidad's industrial capital based on a vibrant petrochemical industry. Couva has evolved both culturally and dynamically over the years, contributing to its rich culture, history and heritage.

This brief historical account of old Couva will cover pre-Columbian times through the period of Spanish rule from 1498 to 1797, the year when the British seized control of Trinidad. It will examine how the foregoing seminal developments have had a profound impact on the socio-economic history of Couva. It will also briefly cover the renaissance of Couva as a village and its evolution into a modern town.

CHAPTER 2

This chapter walks the readers through the historical developments taking place in Trinidad, right from the beginning. It started well before the discovery of Trinidad by Columbus. Who were the pre-Columbian migrant settlers of Trinidad? What do we know regarding how they lived? The chapter discusses the history of various pre-ceramic tribes and agro-ceramic tribes that migrated to Trinidad, followed by the Arawak and Carib tribes and ends at the first settlers of Couva.

FIRST PEOPLES: TRINIDAD AND COUVA

To appreciate the local historical developments in Couva, it is important to understand the history of the island.

Christopher Columbus "discovered" Trinidad in 1498 on his third voyage to the New World. He named it after the Trinity and claimed it as a possession of the Spanish Crown. Columbus chronicled in his log his observations of the island, stating glowingly, "There were houses and people, fine cultivated land, as green and lovely as the orchards of Valencia in March" (Cohen, 1969, p. 210). During his discovery of Trinidad, Columbus first encountered the Indians of the southwestern part of the island called Icacos Point. The Indians made contact with Columbus when a group armed with bows, arrows and wooden shields paddled out in a canoe and communicated with him, cautiously keeping their distance. He tried to make friends with them, by having his men perform a dance upon one of his ship's deck, but they misunderstood

4

this gesture as a warlike demonstration and responded with a volley of arrows aimed at the strange visitors. Columbus, though, described the Indians favourably, recording:

> ...[T]hey were all young, well built and not black but fairer than the other natives I have seen in the Indies. They were handsome, with fine limbs and bodies, and long straight hair cut in the Spanish manner, and round their heads they wore a cotton cloth elaborately patterned in colours, which I believed to be *almaizares* [i.e., Moorish headdresses]. They wore another of these scarves round their body in place of breeches. (Cohen, 1969, p. 210)

At the time of discovery, the island was inhabited by three main Indian tribes: the Caribs, Arawaks and the Nepuyos. (In this work, the Indians will be called Amerindians generally, except where specificity is more appropriate.)

Spanish colonists established a permanent settlement at St. Joseph in 1592 after previously failed attempts. The colonisation of Trinidad, however, actually dates back to before the arrival of the Spaniards to the island.

The Amerindians were the first settlers of Trinidad who reached the island after migrating from South America. Unlike Columbus, they can validly claim that they were actually the first to discover the island. They were expert navigators and used their handmade canoes to travel across the ocean to the island. The Amerindians called the island *Iere*, meaning *the land of the humming bird* (Grant, 1923, p. 45), although some claim that the true name the indigenes gave to the country was *Kairi*, meaning *Island* (Hollis, 1941, p. 6).

PRE-COLUMBIAN MIGRANT SETTLERS

Trinidad's history predates the arrival of Columbus. In fact, during the pre-Columbian period, various cultural and ethnic tribes from

South America migrated to Trinidad in waves at different times, which is evident from archaeological discoveries. Starting with simple pre-agro-ceramic Archaic migrant groups, there were subsequent immigrant tribes who brought a more sophisticated agro-ceramic culture to the region.

Evidence of the existence of humans in Trinidad dates back 7,000 years. The first group to inhabit the island was an Archaic tribe called the Ortoiroids who began to arrive in about 5,000 B.C. The earliest human remains, named the ***Banwari man,*** were discovered in Banwari Trace in Oropouche in southwestern Trinidad. These remains date back to 5,000 B.C. (Reid, 2009, p. 16). This evidence points to the existence of this Archaic tribe. It is assumed that they migrated to Trinidad from the Orinoco region, when Trinidad was reportedly once attached to the South American mainland. Those were the first Trinidadians who inhabited the area until around 250 B.C.

The Ortoiroids' cultural tradition was pre-ceramic (i.e., non-pottery making). They were simple nomadic hunter-gatherers and basic toolmakers. Their tools were made from stone and/or shells. The common stone tools included manos, mutates, pestles, simple choppers, hammer stones, and chipped stone, and most were likely imported from other neighbouring areas. They designed jewellery made of animal teeth. Artefacts included spear points and barbs. The traditional notion that the Ortoiroids were a pre-agro-ceramic group is now being challenged by recent archaeological evidence, which indicates that they were indeed potters and planters.

The Ortoiroids were followed by the Saladoid tribe, who were characterised by ceramic making, horticulture, and sedentary settlements. It is believed that they originated in South America and travelled to the island of Trinidad in canoes in 500 B.C., and then later spread northward to other Caribbean islands. They were hunters, mollusc collectors, fishers and farmers, manioc cultivators, and brought their polytheistic and animistic religion to Trinidad. The Saladoid cultural tradition made ornate pottery in a distinctive style of white-on-red and zone-incised-cross hatching. Their society was arguably egalitarian in nature. They lived in villages, which surrounded a square that was used for ritual and ceremonial events. The tribe settled in various locations on the island until around 600 A.D. Saladoid sites have been found in Blanchisseuse in the north and Erin in the south (Reid, 2009, pp. 17-29).

Other groups who migrated after the Saladoids were also agro-ceramic tribes. Following the Saladoids, the Barrancoids, who apparently travelled from Venezuela to the island, settled in villages along Trinidad's southern coast around 350 A.D. During their migration to various places, they may have either displaced or bypassed the Saladoids' communities. They were expert canoeists and possibly long-distance traders. The tribe may have dwelt among the Saladoids with whom they inter-married or interacted. Their culture faded around 650 A.D. (Reid, 2009, pp. 29-32).

The Barrancoids were succeeded by the Arauquinoids, who were called *Guayabitoid* in Trinidad, around 650 A.D. They also emigrated from South America and occupied the coastal areas of the island.

Finally, in about 1300 A.D., the Mayoids arrived on Trinidad from South America, and thereafter, they became the dominant tribe. This period, of course, is shortly before the arrival of Columbus. This last group included the Caribs and Arawaks and other tribes who were present at the time of European contact with Trinidad's tribes.

ARAWAKS AND CARIBS

Arawaks were peaceful people, which points to the fact that these Savaneta settlers were likely of the Arawak tribal culture based on their friendly and hospitable nature. They welcomed the Catholic missionaries, cooperated with them and gave their input in the setting up and building of a religious mission. The Tribe also named the region after an Arawakan word, *Cuba*, which furthers the notion that they were likely from the Arawak tribal culture.

Typically, the Arawak was an agro-ceramic producing tribe that used stone tools. Their food sources were fishing, farming, and hunting. The Arawaks likely practised shifting agriculture and they developed a basic agricultural technique called **conucos,** which consisted of man-made mounds of earth covered with leaves. The leaves improved drainage in the mounds and protected them from soil erosion. The principal agricultural tool employed by the Arawaks was the digging stick. They planted various crops on these mounds, including their main crop manioc, along with sweet potatoes, yams, and *tania*. Crops like corn, beans, cotton, tobacco, calabash, pepper, and squash were also grown. These secondary crops were planted along the margins of the mounds or in a separate area. They made bread from their cassava produce, and tobacco was commonly used in religious ceremonies.

The Arawaks used a spear, hook and line, and net for fishing. The Amerindians in Trinidad used the bow extensively for hunting wild animals for meat, and they possibly set traps to catch small game.

The Amerindians were skilled canoe-makers and expert navigators. Canoes were made from large, tall trees, which were chopped down and then dug out, with burning used to assist in further hollowing out. Canoes were used for travel, communication, and fishing and trading (i.e., bartering). We know that the Savaneta inland Amerindian community frequented the coast, as evident from distinct Indian dirt footpaths, which are shown on old maps of the island. These paths probably became paved roads in modern times, running from the coastal region to the interior of Couva.

Amerindians used tools made of stone, wood, and bone. Most of their stone tools were obtained through trade with other South American tribes, as they were made of stone not native to Trinidad. They were proficient with basic weapons: the bow and arrow, spear, club and dart.

Amerindians lived simple lives. Their houses were made of wooden posts and the roofs and walls were covered with palm leaves. *Caciques'* (i.e., tribal leaders) houses were rectangular and much larger than the houses of the normal members of the village whose houses were generally bell-shaped. The bell shape may have resembled an 'A' shape where the upper part was probably to be used as an attic for resting. Houses were shared, and each house could possibly accommodate between 12 and 60 persons (Glazier, 1980 p. 154).

The principal artisan craft of Amerindians was pottery making, mostly bowls and cassava griddles. The pottery of the Mayoids was made until the 18th century. It was tempered exclusively with *caraipe*, i.e., the burnt bark of the *kwepi* tree, which is widespread in Trinidad. The usual shape of their pottery was a necked jar, only decorated with a tiny punctuated or nicked rim or wall knobs and occasionally black painted rims (Sued-Badillo, 2003, p. 186).

The wooden or clay bowl was used for food preparation and serving, and the carved-out calabash was used as a vessel for drinking water.

Other artisan crafts included spinning cotton and weaving cloth from it, button and needle making from bone, weaving baskets from straw, and making carved-back wood stools. Coarser fibres were used to make fishing lines, nets, and hammocks.

Amerindians painted their bodies. They went nude except for a simple loincloth. Their jewellery was made from wood, coral, shell, stone and bone. Gold jewellery was imported, and so was the gold crown worn by the *cacique*. Their hair was well cropped, and they practised good personal hygiene. Amerindians had a lot of free time, and as part of their leisure activities, they played a ball game in an open village court.

Typically, the Arawakan village, located near a riverbank, was headed by a *cacique*, who was assisted by military leaders and a shaman or priest in leading the clan. It was the first form of local governance on the island. The priest cared for the villagers' spiritual and medical needs. They would communicate with their gods and spirits on behalf of the society's members by purifying themselves and then becoming intoxicated by smoking a form of tobacco. The women's role in the village included growing, tending and harvesting of crops, domestic activities, weaving, and pottery making. Men were responsible for hunting, fishing and fighting. Arawakan village society in Trinidad was apparently not organised in a hierarchical structure.

Certainly, the negative characterisation of Amerindian peoples by Europeans is a historical falsity, pure ignorance or cultural bias. Dissenting from the negative stereotyping of the indigenes, Canadian Presbyterian Minister, Kenneth J. Grant (1923), remarked, "They are described as well-formed people, brave, living in primitive simplicity

9

and yet not wholly ignorant of the arts, particularly that of weaving cotton into cloth" (pp. 48-49).

Their Carib counterparts, on the contrary, could be fierce and aggressive. Unlike the settled society of the Arawaks, the Caribs were a more mobile tribe. They often took to raiding, looting and burning the villages of the peaceful and hospitable Arawaks. In their raids, they seized Arawaks and sold them as slaves to European colonists in the New World. They were hostile to Europeans, forcefully resisting attempts to colonise the island and attacking their embryonic settlements.

SAVANETA'S FIRST SETTLERS

Since the Amerindians were Trinidad's first peoples, it is not surprising that they were also the first group to inhabit Savaneta (Couva). In fact, Savaneta was one of the many sites in Trinidad that the Amerindians inhabited. Savaneta has many Archaic sites. While a full archaeological exploration is yet to be done, Yale University archaeologist, Irving Rouse, described the site as "a scattered deposit of flint chips" and a likely workshop of Archaic (Ortoiroid) Amerindians (Ray, 2015, p. 13). Subsequent cultural groups certainly inhabited Savaneta. This indicates that Amerindians inhabited Couva thousands of years ago.

(Reportedly, in the nearby Cascajal region, the Chaima Indians inhabited Carapichaima Village and apparently, Amerindians settled in California Village in Savaneta during an unknown period. Meanwhile, other Indians settled in the Tortuga-Mayo area, which is in close proximity to Savaneta.)

In 1687, Savaneta was a site of Amerindian settlement. We know this from the Spanish Capuchin missionaries that met a group of 34 Amerindians who lived there. Apparently, the Amerindians were directly entrusted to a Spanish lord and lived in an *encomienda*, as will be evident later, but it may not have been a formal village.

The Amerindian group that inhabited Savaneta was strategically situated near one of the area's rivers, a source of potable water and freshwater fish. (Additionally, there was scattered tribal habitation along Savaneta's Paria coast, which provided marine resources for nourishment and survival needs.) The habitation site was located a few miles inland from Savaneta's coast—perhaps because of Spanish raids on Amerindian communities directly on the coast—but still permitting easy access to the exploitation of marine resources. The sedimentary soil found near the riverbanks, as well as the physical lay of the land, would have been favourable for agriculture. The undulating land found in the area provided generally good drainage for the soil. The existence of a variety of fauna and flora near the riverbanks presented a good source for collecting and hunting activities. These earliest immigrants occupied the eastern part of Savaneta, as they inhabited the area. That eastern portion now includes the modern-day villages of Indian Trail and Milton, situated at the base of the Montserrat Hills. It was the fertile land, the abundance of fish in the rivers, and the copious resources of Savaneta that were attractive for Amerindians settlement. Before the imposition of the purported *encomienda* system in Couva, the local Amerindians would have engaged in traditional economic practices.

Carib Indian Family by John G. Stedman, 1818
The Picture Art Collection/Alamy Stock Photos
Reproduced with permission

CHAPTER 3

This chapter continues with the history of Couva following the Amerindian period. Trinidad was subjected to Spanish colonisation and it became a source of slave labour for other Spanish colonies. And Couva's natives were at risk of being captured and made slaves. Learn about how the people of Trinidad were labelled as "cannibals" by the Spanish Crown and how Juan Bono took advantage of the Indians. Walk through the history and find out how Las Casas exposed the mistreatment of the Indians in the Spanish colonies, which led to the passing of the *New Laws of the Indies for the Good Treatment and Preservation of the Indians* and their impact on the lives of the Indians.

MISTREATMENT OF NATIVES

After the Amerindians, the Spaniards founded a settlement in Trinidad. First, the island had to be conquered before it could be settled. From the very beginning, Spain's policy was one of disinterest towards Trinidad because it did not offer reserves of gold and silver, although it was much later discovered that Couva does have rich iron deposits (Joseph, 1838/1970, p. 9.). Thus, there was no urgency or benefit to conquest, thereby resulting in its underdevelopment—economically and religiously. Instead, Spain's interest was focussed on other treasure-rich lands in the New World such as Mexico and Peru, depending on them to fill its coffers with precious metals. Following Columbus' discoveries, Spain swiftly granted charters to Spanish explorers to colonise the New

World. Called *conquistadores* (i.e., conquistadors), these explorers were military men who were inspired by tales of treasure in the new lands and became motivated to go there to seek gold, glory, land, and souls to convert to Roman Catholicism. To achieve their goals, they had to conquer and subjugate the natives of the newly discovered lands by waging war against any who resisted.

Trinidad, nevertheless, possessed one major attraction to Spain: a large population of Amerindians. Consequently, the island became a source of slave labour for other Spanish colonies. In 1503, Queen Isabella of Spain declared that "cannibals" of the Caribbean, who resisted the colonists and the Catholic faith, might be captured and sold as slaves in other parts of the Spanish dominion or elsewhere. The Spanish Crown gave in to pressure from the colonists in Hispaniola (now Haiti and the Dominican Republic) who needed more labourers, and issued the *Real Cedula* of December 23, 1511, which declared that the Caribs of Trinidad were cannibals, and their capture and enslavement were authorised (Thomas, 2003, p. 296; Whitehead, 1984, p. 70). Spanish ship captains sailed to Trinidad and captured Amerindians, only to export them to the Spanish Caribbean colonies of Puerto Rico and Hispaniola, where they were enslaved in mines and agriculture, (Thomas, 2003, p. 296) or in the pearl grounds of Margarita and Cubagua (Matthews, 1953, p. 14).

Members of the Spanish *audiencia* (court of justice) of Hispaniola coveted Indian slave labourers as their island's native population was rapidly dying out. The members, who also possessed administrative power, showed careless disregard for the rights of the natives, partly because they benefited from the Indian slave trade, slavery and, as mentioned later, the *encomienda* system (Tenenbaum, 1999, p. 77; Thomas, 2003, p. 381).

To obtain slaves, members of the *audiencia* collaborated with ship captains to capture Indians. One such captain was Juan Bono de Quejo. In 1516, the members approved a flotilla, which was commanded by Bono, to sail from Hispaniola with about 50 to 60 men destined for Trinidad to bring back natives (Thomas, 2003, p. 381; Williams, 1973, p. 4). While sojourning there, he used violence and deceit to capture the island's natives. Spanish historian Bartholomew de Las Casas (1542/2008) reported on the horrific kidnapping perpetrated by Bono. According to him, Bono employed a sinister plan to kidnap Amerindians of Trinidad. He pretended in front of the island's inhabitants that he had come in peace and friendship to live amongst them. In turn, the Amerindians reciprocated with their hospitality. They provided Bono with food during his sojourn. The Spaniards made the Amerindians build a large house for them (the Amerindians) to live in. When the building was near completion, Bono lured 400 of them into the building to see its progress. Betraying the trust of the Indians, his men, with their arms in hand, surrounded the building. Bono demanded that the entrapped Indians surrender. Some did and were captured; others resisted and were wounded or massacred. Still, 100 men escaped; they grabbed their arms and took refuge in another house of their own, ready to defend themselves. Bono and his men now surrounded this house of refuge. When they refused to surrender, he set the house on fire, killing all inside. Bono, the brute and slaver, then set sail with his captured Amerindian loot and sold them as slaves in Puerto Rico and Hispaniola (pp. 62-63).

The unrelenting slave raids resulted in a thinning out of Trinidad's indigenous population. Hence, Savaneta's Amerindians, especially those on the coast, were at risk of being kidnapped and made slaves in other Spanish colonies.

Not only were the Trinidad Amerindians unfairly declared cannibals, they were also branded as "idolaters". Ironically, the Spanish conquerors of Latin America and the Caribbean were themselves idolaters too: they idolized gold and silver, for their discoveries of large quantities of these precious metals brought them great riches.

PROTECTOR OF THE INDIANS

In conquering the Caribbean islands, the Spanish *conquistadores* committed genocide, enslavement and other cruel acts against the indigenous people. Conquest meant destroying the native Indian society. Some Spanish observers criticised the genocide and inhumane treatment and the destruction of the Indians by the conquerors. Among them were members of the Dominican religious order who were the most outspoken and consistent critics. These clerics found their greatest spokesman in one of their own members, Bartholomew de Las Casas who subsequently joined their order (Rogozinski, 1992, pp. 31-32).

In colonising the New World, the Spaniards, in the early 16th century, transplanted to the new lands their Old World *encomienda system*—a system similar to feudalism. Under this *encomienda* system, an allotment of Indian residents was entrusted to conquerors. The grantees of the *encomiendas* (i.e., *encomenderos*) were agricultural *entrepreneurs* and miners. The Indians lived in villages located on their estates (Watters, 1937, p. 131). Under this system, Indians were required to pay a tribute (i.e., a type of payment) in the form of either food or money or made to work for the *encomenderos*. In return, they were offered military protection from invading tribes, promised the teaching of the tenets of Christianity, and the European way of life for their good welfare. Nevertheless, the owners defaulted on their promises to teach the Indians about the Roman Catholic faith. Instead, the *encomienda* system had devolved essentially into a form of Indian slavery, under which they were exploited and abused.

Las Casas himself was granted an *encomienda* of Indian serfs, thereby becoming an *encomendero*. But then he became a priest and later a Dominican monk. He witnessed the atrocities committed against the Indians by the *conquistadores* and participated in the conquest of Cuba in 1512. Appalled by what he witnessed, Las Casas exposed the *conquistadores* and *encomenderos'* mistreatment of the natives in the Spanish colonies in the New World.

To address the brutal mistreatment of the indigenous people by the Spanish conquistadors, Spain issued the Laws of Burgos (1512). The laws prohibited abuse of the natives, but supported their conversion to the Roman Catholic faith. Rarely were these laws enforced, however, thereby rendering them useless in preventing the abuse that the natives had to face.

Growing deeply troubled by the brutal mistreatment of the Indians, Las Casas renounced his *encomienda* in 1515, which he considered a form of slavery, and denounced the brutality of *conquistadores* and *encomenderos* and devoted himself to defending the natives. Las Casas criticised the enslavement of the Indians because it caused the dispersion of their villages and the division of their families (Matthews, 1953, p. 16).

Las Casas became a fierce human rights crusader who publicised the mistreatment of the Indians in Spanish colonies and advocated that the Indians deserved to be treated as humans. He was determined to bring about change through his vocal advocacy, shaming of the perpetrators, his writings and the enactment of legislation. In 1515, Las Casas took his Indian humanitarian cause to King Charles I of Spain who then appointed him as the *Protector of the Indians.* In 1519, the King of Spain ordered the Spanish colonists to refrain from using force against the Indians they governed. But the order did not prevent the continuing mistreatment of the Indians.

Influenced by Las Casas, the Spanish Crown passed the *New Laws of the Indies for the Good Treatment and Preservation of the Indians* in 1542 and 1543. The new laws abolished Indian slavery, which was a big step. It also banned the *encomienda* system, forbade the demand of free labour by the *encomenderos,* and ordered that the natives be treated fairly. Although the Spanish Crown had stepped in to protect the Indians, these new laws were ignored by the Spanish colonists and they violently resisted them. The Spanish Crown caved in and suspended many parts of the more unpopular laws, including the abolition of the *encomienda* system, which the colonists saw as a means of weakening their power over their Indian labourers and causing their economic ruin. Slowly, however, the Spanish Crown started arranging to phase out the *encomienda* system and to replace it with other systems.

As one aspect of his human rights campaign, Las Casas defended the Trinidad Amerindians. As stated before, he had publicised the kidnappings and other diabolical atrocities committed against them by the Spaniard slavers, and spoke out about these abuses, calling the unconscionable perpetrators *tyrants.* Fighting for the natives of Trinidad, Las Casas persuaded the Spanish King's council to declassify Trinidad as a Carib country in 1518 to avert a declaration of war against them, at least temporarily, as he informed the council that the inhabitants were not cannibals.

The Spanish authorities indeed found out that the island's inhabitants were not cannibals, but just very quiet people (Helps, 1856, p. 32).

Bartolome De Las Casas (1474-1566).
Spanish missionary and historian.
Saran Images/Granger.
Reproduced with permission.

CHAPTER 4

The Spanish authorities had just learned that the island's inhabitants were not cannibals after all. Learn about the various governors that were appointed in Trinidad and how the island was left without a "permanent" governor for almost a century. Don Antonio de Berrio began his journey towards Trinidad and this opened a new chapter in the history of the island. But Antonio de Berrio's occupation of Trinidad was illegal. Learn how the future of Trinidad and the Indians was shaped post-de Berrio's family regimes and the raid of Trinidad by Raleigh. Read about the miserable state of the island, the establishment of the *encomendia* system, and the planting of lucrative tobacco and cocoa crops that temporarily reprieved the inhabitants from their misery. This chapter also sheds light on the exploitation of the island by various European powers, and the many developmental setbacks it had to face because of all these invasions.

THE SPANISH SETTLEMENT

The Spaniards had made sporadic attempts to establish a permanent Spanish settlement in Trinidad. In 1520, the Spanish Crown named Don Roderigo de Bastidas as the Governor of Trinidad, but his nomination was forcefully opposed by Columbus's son, Don Diego Columbus—who had been the Governor of Santo Domingo—on the grounds that the nomination breached an agreement with his father. As a result, Roderigo de Bastidas withdrew from the nomination. It took ten years thereafter for another governor to be commissioned. In 1530, the Spanish Crown appointed Don Antonio Sedeno, who had been the Royal Treasurer of San Juan, as the Governor of Trinidad. Sedeno received a commission to conquer and colonise the island peacefully, pacify and Christianise the natives and build a fort. Although he did encounter hostile Caribs in one part of Trinidad, he had developed a friendly relationship with the Amerindians who were living in the south of the island. Nevertheless, it was mainly because of his disagreement with his Spanish colleagues on the South American mainland that his tenure was unsuccessful. He died in 1538 (Hollis, 1941, p. 8).

With no urgency to conquer Trinidad, the forgotten island languished without a governor for another three decades. In 1571, Don Juan Ponce de Leon was commissioned as the Governor of the island and was instructed again to peacefully reduce (i.e., congregate into settlements), and convert the Amerindians, preserve them and to lay the foundation of towns as well. However, in a short span of time after landing, the hostility of the Amerindians, together with the illnesses his group contracted due to the island's overall unhealthy conditions, caused his mission to be abandoned (Hollis, 1941, p. 8).

It was not easy to colonise Trinidad. The failed efforts of Sedeno and Ponce De Leon offer clear evidence of this fact.

However, the island's history was bound to change.

In 1592, Don Antonio de Berrio, the Spanish Provincial Governor of Guayana, Dorado, and Manoa, who claimed the governorship of the island as heir to his wife's uncle, Don Gonzales Ximenes de Quesada, Conquistador of New Granada, commanded Domingo de Vega to go to Trinidad and colonise it. De Vega landed with a party of 30 men at what is today called Mucurapo, an area just west of Port of Spain. He planted a cross and then informed the Amerindians he met there that he was taking possession of the island in the name of the Spanish Crown (which ironically it always was since 1498). The reasons he put forth were to bring them Light and Faith, to prevent their capture and sale as slaves, and to protect them from the murderous raids of the Caribs from other islands. Trusting his words, the Amerindians promised allegiance to the Spanish Crown (Hollis, 1941, pp. 9-10).

Following de Vega's announcement to the Amerindians at Mucurapo, he sailed up the Caroni River and founded the town of

St. Joseph (the original capital of Trinidad) as a permanent settlement (Trinidad Historical Society, n.d., p. 3).

This time the endeavour would prove to be successful.

The town was founded on land granted by Guanaguanare, one of the *caciques* of the Amerindian nations that existed on the island. De Vega constructed a church, a Governor's house, a Cabildo to administer the town's affairs and a prison (Hollis, 1941, pp. 10-11).

Before taking up residence in St. Joseph, de Berrio had harboured an open obsession with finding El Dorado, the mythical South American city of gold, and had conducted at least three expeditions to locate it. When de Vega arrived in Trinidad, he also began to prepare Trinidad as a base from which de Berrio could continue his quest for El Dorado and as a supply depot for South American provinces. De Berrio took up residence on the island in early 1593. After his arrival, he scoured the land for provisions and partitioned it into estates, which he distributed to his troops (Hanson, 1967, pp. 230-235). In 1593, de Berrio took a census of the island's population and it numbered 35,000 (Newson, 1976, p. 31)

COLUMBUS: TRINIDAD, 1498. Christopher Columbus and his men discovering the three-peaked island of Trinidad (top left) in 1498. Engraving, 1730.

De Berrio's occupation of Trinidad had been illegal, and Francisco de Vides who had officially received a contract of settlement of the island in 1592 challenged it. Spain's Council of the Indies decreed in January 1594 that de Berrio must quit the island (The Trinidad Historical Society, n.d., para. 2). But he ignored the order. Instead, he sent Domingo de Vega to Spain to vindicate his possession of the island to the Spanish Crown (Hollis, 1941, pp. 9-10).

RALEIGH'S RAID AND DEVELOPMENT SETBACKS

However, the island suffered ongoing developmental setbacks. In 1595, Sir Walter Raleigh invaded St. Joseph. This was an attempt to avenge the luring and subsequent killing of a group of English sailors by de Berrio and his troops while they were on a visit to Trinidad the year before. In addition, this attack was also planned to obtain information from the Spaniards on the island about Guiana and de Berrio's El Dorado enterprise.

Raleigh arrived in March of 1595 and anchored off the coast at Icacos Point. A few days later, he sailed to the Port of Spain where he was received cordially by Spaniards who traded and socialised with him. He was able to extract some valuable information about Guiana from them. Raleigh also developed friendly relations with the Amerindians, and he was informed by one of them about the troop reinforcements de Berrio had requested from Margarita and Cumana. De Berrio banned the Amerindians from dealing with Raleigh. Regardless of the risk of being put to death by the Governor, the Amerindians nevertheless met Raleigh nightly and complained lamentably of the cruelty of de Berrio, how he had dispossessed them of their land and allotted every one of his soldiers a part and imprisoned their *caciques*.

Before the additional troops could arrive in Trinidad, Raleigh pre-emptively attacked de Berrio's *Corp de guard* in the evening and put them to the sword. Then he and his troops advanced onwards, and by daybreak, they captured the new town of St. Joseph. Raleigh chillingly discovered for himself the tyranny of de Berrio who had enslaved five Amerindian *caciques* (*kings*), put them in chains, and starved and tortured them. So he (Raleigh) immediately liberated them. But he didn't stop there. At the urging of the Amerindians, he set the town on fire! Before leaving Port of

Spain for Icacos Point, Raleigh addressed all of the island's Amerindian leaders (who were enemies to the Spaniards), revealing to them that he was sent by the great *Cacique* of the North (i.e., Queen Elizabeth I of England) to set them free from Spaniard tyranny and oppression (see *Text Box*)(Raleigh (1596/1887, pp. 11-20).

Once again, de Berrio's rule demonstrates the betrayal of trust of the Amerindians regarding the promises made to them by de Vega and the tyrannical rule foisted on the Amerindians, similar to the tyranny of the slavers and colonisers that Las Casas, the Protector of the Indians, had criticised so vociferously. While Las Casas sought to free Indians from tyranny by speaking out and obtaining the help of the Spanish Crown to bring about reforms to protect them, Raleigh fought to free them militarily on behalf of his Queen. Savaneta's Amerindians, even though living in a remote area, were still under the iron fist of de Berrio's rule. And Raleigh had come to free them from that tyranny and oppression too.

**Sir Walter Raleigh sets at Liberty five Indian
Kings, who were all linked together.**
J. Cooke, Publisher. London, 1770.
Courtesy of the John Carter Brown Library

Raleigh's Address to Trinidad's Captains (Caciques)

We then hastened away towards our purposed discovery, and first I called all the captains of the island together that were enemies to the Spaniards, for there were some which Berreo had brought out of other countries, and planted there to eat out and waste those that were natural of the place; and by my Indian interpreter, which I carried out of England, I made them understand that I was the servant of a queen, who was the great Cazique of the north, and a virgin, and had more Caziqui under her than there were trees in their island; that she was an enemy to the Castellani [i.e., the Spaniards] in respect of their tyranny and oppression, and that she delivered all such nations about her as were by them oppressed, and having freed all the coast of the northern world from their servitude, had sent me to free them also, and withal to defend the country of Guiana from their invasion and conquest. I showed them her Majesty's picture, which they so admired and honoured as it had been easy to have brought them idolatrous thereof. - Raleigh

Raleigh took de Berrio and his lieutenant (Alvaro Jorge) "prisoners" aboard his ship (Hollis, 1941, p. 18). The British explorer had been on a quest to discover El Dorado and had hoped that de Berrio, whom he treated as an honoured guest, would be an oracle who would supply him with valuable information about that elusive city. Unfortunately, Raleigh's mission failed after several months of explorations and he set sail for England, releasing de Berrio in June 1595 to resume his governorship. De Berrio, instead, became an absentee governor, took up residence along the banks of the Orinoco River, and continued his dogged mission to find El Dorado. However, he disappointingly never realised his dream of discovering it. In fact, his mission turned out to be nothing but a grand illusion.

While de Berrio was away on this latest expedition, Felipe de Santiago under the instructions of Francisco de Vides seized the opportunity to land on the island. He rebuilt St. Joseph. At that time, Domingo de Vega, who apparently had been away from the island on official business, made an incursion into the island and retook the town on behalf of the new governor, Fernando de Berrio, who had succeeded his father, Antonio de Berrio, who died in Guiana in 1597. The Spanish Crown had sanctioned the re-entry of de Vega into Trinidad because it feared Raleigh's announced intention to return and occupy the island.

During his brief stay in Trinidad, Raleigh had observed the composition of the island's Amerindian population. He found that there were five groups at the time: the Iaio (Yao), the Arawaca, the Salvaios, the Nepuyos, and the Carinepagatos (a Carib-speaking tribe). All of them had settlements in the Guianas, South America as well.

In the early part of the 17th century, Spain introduced the *encomienda* in the island, as part of its administrative system, after the colonists were settled. Many *encomiendas* (containing Amerindian villages) were granted to Spaniard colonists in Trinidad, but only four located in the northern part of the island—Arauca (Arouca), Tacarigua, Caura, and Aricagua (San Juan)—were continuously operational until 1716 when they were abolished. It was reported that de Berrio had granted 70 *encomiendas* (Newson, 1976, pp. 153-154). It is likely that at one time Savaneta had been a part of the *encomienda* system because reportedly the Amerindians in that area had been directly entrusted to a Spanish lord.

Through the *encomendia* system, the Spaniard colonists developed an agricultural economy on the island. They grew tobacco, which brought a good measure of prosperity to Trinidad. But Spain continued to neglect the island and failed to send ships there for long periods of time. The island all but disappeared from Spain's scope and its inhabitants were obliged to supply themselves on their own (Bottcher, 2007, p. 158), resorting to the smuggling trade with foreigners to survive. The island's residents traded tobacco with the Dutch in violation of Spain's monopolistic trade policy. As a result, the Spanish Crown snuffed out this profitable trade. Governors requested supplies and additional troops to strengthen the island's defence, but were ignored. The island languished again. It remained impoverished, underdeveloped, sparsely populated and poorly fortified.

In the 1640s, English planters attempted to settle in Trinidad (Hollis, 1941, p. 49). Next, the Dutch invaded the island in 1640 and captured St Joseph. Once more, British troops, this time led by Sir Tobias Bridges, attacked the island in 1672. Finally, in 1677 French forces commanded by Marquis de Maintenon invaded and plundered the colony (De Verteuil, 1884, pp. 428-429). According to Trinidad historian de Verteuil (1884), "The progress of the island was thus arrested, and great misery prevailed" (p. 429).

These worrisome problems exacerbated the island's already miserable state. Nonetheless, the residents enjoyed a reprieve when they turned to the cultivation of cocoa. About the year 1678, the Spanish colonists in Trinidad earnestly devoted their energies towards growing cocoa as a crop. As the industry developed, it brought prosperity to the island once again (Hollis, 1941, p. 67). But catastrophic events were yet to come.

Walter Raleigh's capture of Trinidad Governor de Berrio during a raid on an island in 1595.

Granger — All rights reserved. Reproduced with permission.

Between Governor Fernando de Berrio's initial rule which ended in 1614 and the appointment of Governor Chacon in 1784, Spain appointed over two and one half dozen governors to Trinidad but owing to severe restrictions on trade and immigration, the island's commercial progress was handicapped and its population increased very slowly (Grant, 1923, p. 50). Smuggling was prevalent, as well. In 1640, the Spanish Governor reported to his King that there were only a few settlers left and they were continually talking about abandoning the island (Hollis, 1941, p. 48). Only in the 1770s did the Spanish Crown take a serious interest in the development of Trinidad. Lack of development of Trinidad seen through the lenses of the Amerindians, however, was a good thing, for development via colonisation meant their dispossession, oppression, and destruction.

CHAPTER 5

This chapter describes the Christianisation efforts directed at the Amerindians of Trinidad. However, these efforts were limited to the urban areas and the village of Port of Spain. Learn about how early missionaries' efforts to Christianise the Amerindians were made to be in vain by some Spanish slavers. This chapter also discusses the Pope's desire to Christianise the natives of the New World and the actions taken by the Spanish King Philip IV against the abuse of Indians. Congregation, conversion, and, ultimately, control of the Amerindians were the chief objectives of the Spanish Crown. Learn about the Royal *Cedula* (1686) addressed to the Governor of Trinidad and Guyana to extend all possible assistance to promote the holy and important work of Capuchin missionaries and to see to it that the Amerindians were congregated into missions and villages.

MISSIONARY EVANGALISATION

Spanish missionaries of Roman Catholic religious orders came to the Caribbean when Columbus explored the area. It was the official policy of Spain to spread the Holy Catholic Faith by converting the "pagans" of newly colonised lands into devout Catholics. The attempts to spread Christianity among the Amerindians of Trinidad were, like the colonisation efforts of the Spaniards, sporadic. These intermittent initiatives did not work or flourish in Trinidad.

The Roman Catholic Franciscan order planted the first seeds of missionary activity in the island. In 1513, a pair of clerics consisting of Friar Francisco de Cordova and a layman, Juan Garces, was sent to teach the Amerindians about the Christian faith and to explain to them the way of salvation. They planned to converse with the locals and determine the most convenient places to build some monasteries on the island. This missionary venture ended tragically for the two clerics.

Las Casas reported that the Amerindians welcomed them with great affection, joy, and respect, and were also enthusiastically disposed to adopting Christian names. But as the clerics were busy making progress in their evangelism, unknown to them some Spaniard slavers arrived on the island. The slavers deceptively persuaded one of the Amerindian Princes named Alphonsus, along with his Princess wife and about 17 of their subjects, to board their ship to receive baptism, which he was particularly desirous of receiving. As soon as the royal couple and the rest were onboard, the Spaniard rogues took them captive, set sail and then sold them all as slaves. The clerics protested the kidnapping and promised the royal couple's subjects the return of their captured Prince, Princess and their retinue. However, after the clerics' repeated efforts became futile, the Amerindians killed them in revenge, believing that the religious men had been complicit in the fraudulent and despicable plot (Las Casas, 1542/2008, pp. 63-65). This and other such incidents made the Amerindians distrustful of such missionaries from the very start.

Part of the commands given to Sedeno and Ponce de Leon was to convert non-Christians to the Roman Catholic faith, as already noted, but those instructions were not effectuated because their colonising missions failed. Another avenue was tried to Christianise the Amerindians, i.e., by entrusting the task to Trinidad's *encomenderos*. But like the other colonial *encomenderos*, they too reneged to instruct the Amerindians about the Roman Catholic faith.

Many other efforts were launched to convert the Amerindian natives to the Christian faith, but these did not produce any great results. A lack of clergy to serve and funding and a host of other reasons frustrated those attempts. As a result, Christianity did not flourish among the Amerindians.

Savaneta's Amerindians were not touched by these Christianisation efforts because of the area's remoteness and the religious neglect by their Spaniard lord(s). The missionary thrusts were mostly directed at Amerindians living in the north of the island around urban St. Joseph and coastal Port of Spain.

Savaneta is one of those areas in the countryside in the central part of the island that the Spaniards only barely colonised before 1687. Missionaries were sent by the Spanish Crown instead to do so as part of Spain's new policy towards Trinidad in the latter part of the 17ᵗʰ century. Because of the work of missionaries, Spain was able to establish greater contact with the native people. Through these missionaries, Spain's colonisation policy transformed Savaneta (i.e., old Couva) religiously and economically by turning it into an agro-religious mission for the conversion of the Amerindian settlers to the Roman Catholic faith. The Catholic mission lasted for about 107 years.

Ever since the discovery of the Caribbean islands by Columbus, the Popes wanted the natives to be converted to Christianity. The Papal Bull *Inter Caetera* of 1493, which initially divided the world between exploration rivals Spain and Portugal by a line of demarcation, authorised these two nations to spread the Catholic faith, overthrow barbarous nations, and convert the inhabitants living in those non-Christian lands (Pope Alexander VI, p. 61).

Spain's justification for conquering— and mistreating— the natives of the New World was contained in The Requirement of 1510, a Spanish-issued legal document. It stated that the Roman Catholic pope had religious authority over the whole world and Spain had been given political authority over the Americas [i.e., excluding Brazil]. When the conquistadors arrived in lands of the New World, they were required to announce an ultimatum to the natives that they were obligated to submit to Spaniard rule and Christian preaching and teaching and free will conversion. If they submitted, then they would be free from enslavement and forced conversion and they would receive many privileges and exemptions from the Spanish Crown. Otherwise, if they resisted the Spaniard rule, then the conquistadors would wage war against them, they would be forced to convert to Christianity, their families would be enslaved, and their goods would be seized and be subjected to all mischief and damage (Requiremento, 1510, pp. 1-2).

Philip IV, the Spanish King, had recognised the *conquistadores'* abuses of the Indians in his colonies. In 1652, he ordered them to cease their military expeditions against the natives and simultaneously instituted the mission system as a new means of pacifying and "civilising" the colonial natives (Watters, 1937, p. 132).

THE ROYAL *CEDULA* OF 1686

In the 1680s, there were renewed initiatives to convert the Amerindians of Trinidad. Because of the prior abuses of the Indians in the New World by *conquistadores*, including amongst their ilk, the *encomenderos*, the Spanish Crown decided to entrust the spiritual and temporal control of the island's Amerindians to missionaries instead. At the request of Fray Felix de Artizono, Capuchin Father and Apostolic Commissioner of the Province of Cumana (Venezuela), the King Charles II of Spain issued a *cedula*, dated 7 February 1686, granting him permission to take 12 Fathers of the Capuchin Order from Spain for the purpose of establishing new missions in Trinidad to convert the Indians to Catholicism.

The Royal *Cedula* was addressed to Don Sebastian de Roteta, the Governor of Trinidad and Guyana. The governor was ordered to extend all possible assistance to promote the holy and important work of the missionaries and to see to it that the Amerindians were congregated into missions and villages.

The 1686 Royal *Cedula* read, in part, as follows:

> ... I have thought it fit to apprise you, for your guidance and that on your part you may render all the assistance possible to these Friars, helping them in such as a way as may best promote the object of so holy and important a work, seeing to it that as fast as the Indians are subdued they be brought together and incorporated in the Missions and Villages, in order that they may live a political and civil life, [An alternative translation reads, in part: "so that they may learn to live a quiet and civilised life" (The Historical Society of Trinidad and Tobago, n.d., p. 2.)] you helping

these Friars to attain this object, while endeavouring to carry out such a serious matter by all the means possible. And at the same time I command you to visit the places and villages of the Jurisdiction under your government, and communicate with the Indians, without allowing the residents to make use of them, attending only to their instructions; for as they are weak, what they seek to avoid with their flight, is not the Doctrine, but physical work, wherewith they are generally disturbed; regarding which matter I recommend you to be increasingly watchful, as you have been instructed to do by various cedulas, it is being a matter of such weight and conscience.... (United States of Venezuela, 1898, pp. 271-272)

According to the Royal Cedula of 1686, the natives were to be taught Christianity by these missionaries to lead a "civilised" life in missions and villages. However, looking at the big picture, congregation, conversion and, ultimately, control of the Indians in missions and villages were the chief objectives of the Spanish Crown. Usually, Spain's policy was that once the missionaries had accomplished their work, the mission would then be secularised, and the Indians would come under control of the Spanish government.

King Charles II of Spain.
Sarin Images/Granger Collection.
Reproduced with permission.

CHAPTER 6

Learn about the Capuchin missionaries' arrival in St. Joseph to spread Christianity and how they established four missions on the island initially to continue the task of the previous missionaries. Study in detail about the siting of the Saint Anne's Mission in Savaneta and the official founding day of Couva that was recorded by Father Arcangel de Barcelona. Read about the good *encomendero*, Juan de Canas, and his emotional handover of the Amerindians to the missionaries.

ESTABLISHMENT OF THE SAINT ANNE'S MISSION

In August 1687, Catalonian Capuchin monks, who were zealous missionaries, began arriving in St. Joseph determined to spread the Christian gospel among native Amerindians. Prefect Father Thomas de Barcelona and Father R. de Figuerola, both veteran Capuchin missionaries who were based in Cumana, Venezuela where missions had been successfully established, soon after joined the group. On the arrival of these latter two clerics in Trinidad, Prefect Father Thomas de Barcelona was chosen as the leader of the assembled Capuchin team to embark on their missionary undertaking in remoter parts of Trinidad.

A short time after their arrival, the Capuchins began their two-decade-long arduous but rewarding missionary journey in Trinidad. On 13 October 1687, Prefect Father Thomas de Barcelona led a contingent of missionary monks and laypersons in the escort of several Spaniards and an Amerindian guide to survey the island's southern and central regions for the establishment of missions (including villages) (Ottley, 1971, p. 25). They were able to establish four different missions in distant areas of the island, the first in Savanna Grande (now Princes Town), after which there were three more missions founded consecutively in Naparima (now San Fernando), Savaneta (now Couva, as stated before), and the Tortuga-Mayo area in the Montserrat Hills.

The mission in Savaneta—developed amidst its wilderness—was called *Santa Anna de Savaneta* (Saint Anne of Savaneta), while the one founded in the Montserrat Hills was named *Nuestra Senora de Montserrate* (Our Lady of Montserrat). According to Boomert (2016), all four missions were founded among the Nepuyo Amerindians (p. 132). Swedish anthropologist Sevn Loven (1935/2010) believes that the Nepuyos were an Arawak tribe (p. 41).

Prior to the arrival of the missionary party in Savaneta, the Trinidad Governor was ordered by the Spanish King to adequately inform the group of 34 local aboriginals and their leaders of Spain's plan to establish a mission. The governor essentially prepared the native group for a meeting with the missionary party in order to decide on the site for this new mission (including a village). The official committee of Capuchin monks arrived in eastern Couva on 19 October 1687, accompanied by the Spaniard lords of the Amerindians. The group, in collaboration with the Amerindians, immediately began the task of locating the best site for the establishment and maintenance of their mission. They were careful to look for a site that put them in close proximity to their potential Amerindian converts.

The group decided on a spot located on the Savaneta River's left bank because the place was rich in natural resources (Borde, 1876/1982, p. 46). The Savaneta River, a small tributary of the Couva River, passes through the village of Milton. The monks described the spot as a fertile plain due to its location on the bank of a river whose waters were crystal clear and nurtured an abundance of delicious fish. Just like the Amerindians, the Capuchin monks had recognised the copious resources and fertility of the lands of Couva.

The Reverend Father Arcangel de Barcelona (1687)—a member of the ecclesiastical party—recorded the founding event as follows:

We arrived on the 19th [i.e., 19 October 1687] (with some discomfort) to the third location [i.e., Savaneta], thereby beforehand prepared the Indians, 34 in number, for the meeting of the election of a place and the union of the people for civil dwelling. And the place was accepted without looking at it. It just so happened that the swamps, created by the disposition of the flatlands, offered no possible way for us to go and investigate: but the universal sense, belonging as much to the Indians as to the lords who came for our decorum to honour us with their company, those which were experts of said land and the lord of those same Indians, unanimously agreed that this place was the best of all places, as they moved through the pleasant plain, fertile due to its location on the bank of a river whose crystalline waters nurtured in her womb delicious fish in abundance; and as we all said that the other places were good, we were in agreement that this one far exceeded all the others and therefore (there was no other possibility) we said 'yes' to accepting it. (p. 99) (Trans. by Translated.)(Also, see *Manuscript 1*).

Hence, 19 October 1687 should be recognised as the official founding day of Couva.

Apparently, the direct lord of the Amerindians of the Savaneta region had been one Juan de Canas, who was a member of the visiting party. Father Cesareo de Armellada calls him *"El buen encomendero"*, i.e., the good *encomendero*, (de Armellada, 1960, p. 94). Father Arcangel reported that de Canas tearfully handed over his entrusted subjects to the missionaries, acknowledging his failure to provide them with religious doctrine and a priest. In his emotional farewell address, he asked his subjects to respect, serve and love their new lords. De Canas assured his servants that their new saintly lords would love and care for them and lead them to heaven (de Barcelona, 1687, pp. 99-100).

Interestingly, Father Arcangel's reporting reveals that Savaneta may have been an *encomienda*.

Manuscript 1

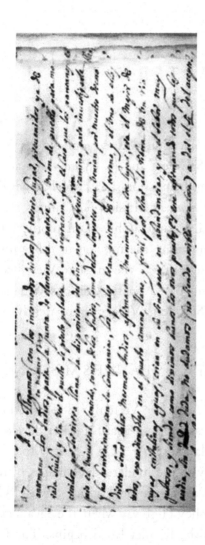

Extract from Father Arcangel de Barcelona's *Viaje desde el Puerto de Cadiz a la Isla de Trinidad y Recorrido de la Misma*, 1687. Diary. Document No. 16. Archives at Arxiu Provincial dels Caputxins de Catalunya, Barcelona

This extract from the manuscript describes the founding of the third Capuchin mission in Trinidad (i.e., Santa Anna de Savaneta in Couva) on 19 October 1687.

CHAPTER 7

This chapter discusses the location of the Saint Anne's Mission on the left bank of a river in Savaneta and its layout in detail. Read about De Verteuil's pinpointing the mission site on the Rivulet Estate, the existence of the apparent *Sabaneta* Mission on Crame's map, the possible identification of the Saint Anne's Church on another map of Trinidad, the Royal Road connecting the mission to other missions and St. Joseph, and Borde's description of the mission. View Leeping's drawing of the mission's layout, based on the author's visualisation. Understand why the modern Savonetta Village is apparently not the site of the Catholic mission.

LOCATION OF THE SAINT ANNE'S MISSION

According to historian L. A. A. De Verteuil (1884), the location of the Saint Anne's Mission was the spot that was later developed as the *Rivulet Estate*—a sugar plantation*(see Map Section 1)*(p. 430). It was situated in close proximity to the modern-day villages of Milton and Indian Trail to the southeast of the present-day town of Couva, adjoining the Sir Solomon Hochoy Highway where the Savaneta River flows through the region and the Rivulet Road begins. The Rivulet Estate no longer exists, and over time, its lands became part of the now defunct Caroni Limited sugar estates. The only element that links the area to the historical existence of Saint Anne's and the Montserrat Mission is the *Mission Road* that passes through Preysal Village nearby.

Historical writings and documents referred to the Saint Anne's Mission as the Savaneta mission or the Sabaneta mission. Maps that were available for this work did not show the explicit words "The Mission of Savaneta", as they do of the Mission of Montserrat. They usually display the single word *Sabaneta.*

The word *Sabaneta,* for example, is shown on a rather interesting map of Trinidad, drawn by military engineer Agustin Crame, in 1777, and titled, *Mapa de la ysla de Trinidad.* A close-up view of the central part of the island seemingly captures the sites of three missions (*see Map Section 1A*). It identifies each mission by, what appears to be, a church-like structure. (The original map is in colour, and shows each structure in red.) Crame features the supposed mission sites of *Monserrate* (Tortuga/Mayo or Montserrat), *Guayria* (San Fernando—which is misplaced) and *Sabaneta* (Savaneta). In reality, central Trinidad had only two missions: Montserrat and Savaneta. It should be noted that Crame's map was drawn at the time when the Savenata Mission had been in operation, although he does not label it *Mission of Sabaneta.*

On this map section, *Sabaneta* is located near to, what appears to be, the left bank of a branch of a Y-shaped river formation which starts near the foothills of Montserrat. As a reminder, Borde stated that the Savaneta mission church was planted on the left bank of the small river Savaneta. This branch or tributary merges with another river, thereafter forming a single river. The single river then courses through, what would be, Savaneta (i.e., Couva) and empties into the Gulf of Paria at *P. d. Cua* (Point of Cua—the last word is spelt almost similar *Cuba,* a word from which Couva is derived). The mouth of the river is labelled *Ostinos* (Oysters), likely indicating the nature of the area. It is evident today that the small Savenata River flows through the Village of Milton and the Y-shaped Savaneta-cum-Couva Rivers are merged rivers. The Savaneta River conjoins the Couva River near the Camden section of Couva, with the merged rivers becoming one river, that is, the Couva River, which then moves through modern Couva and flows into the Gulf. Even today, this area on the coast is laden with oysters. Additionally, Crame distinctly shows a road running from *Monserrate* to *Sabaneta* and then to points northward and a bend in the road or a connection of roads at *Sabaneta*. The direction of and the bend in the road are roughly similar to the ones drawn on other maps, namely, *Map Section 2* and *Map Section 3*—shown later. The red-coloured structure is very likely the Saint Anne's mission church. Crame's *Sabaneta* appears to be the Savaneta Mission, although its location relative to points on the coast is questionable. It could be that the points on the coast are mislabeled.

Nevertheless, another map titled, *Map showing Trinidad Island and adjacent coast of Venezuela*, (circa 1700s), shows a red-coloured church tower, with a cross mounted on top, and is named *Sabanela [sic] M*. The tower is sited in central Trinidad, not too far from a mount in eastern Couva and is located slightly southeast of Point Lisas. This church tower is very likely the Saint Anne's Church at the Savaneta Mission. (A black and white section of this map—perhaps based on Crame's map— is reproduced as *Map Section 1B*.)

What later-published maps do show in the Savaneta area are *Savaneta Indian Village, Savaneta Village Indien, and Indian Village of Savanette*. Presumably, these were the Saint Anne's Mission after it was closed.

On the presumption that the Indian village was the closed mission, maps differ on the precise location of the mission. Both an 1802 British map *(published by Faden)* and a French government map (**circa** 1804) of Trinidad place the mission, labelled *Savaneta Indian Village and Savaneta Village Indien*, respectively, slightly southeast of Couva's Savaneta Point (*see Maps Sections 2 and 3*).

Meanwhile, an 1800 British map of Trinidad *(engraved by Allen and published from actual 1797 surveys)* places the mission (labelled the *Indian Village of Savanette*) slightly northeast of this same point (*see Map section 4*). Nevertheless, the northeast location is in Cascajal and on the right bank of the Cuba River, and hence, is a doubtful site, because the mission church was planted on the left bank of the Savaneta River. Therefore, each of the southeast locations is a more plausible site as they are both in Savaneta and vividly connected by road to the Montserrat Mission.

In Spanish territories in both North America and Latin America, the main road was called *El Camino Real* (the Spanish term for "The Royal Road"). As the name implies, it was a special road because it received royal status and its maintenance was the responsibility of the local Spanish government. It served as the main thoroughfare for transportation, conquering and exploration of new territories, trade and commerce, the ferrying out of plundered treasure, and for the movements of the locals, colonists, government officials, the military, and missionaries. It was traversed by foot, mule, horse, and animal-drawn carts. Parts of the road were paved with stones, while other parts consisted of dirt trails. Often, the Royal Road incorporated old Indian trails. The road connected the administrative centres and ports to far-flung posts, such as *pueblos* (i.e., villages), forts, and missions, in the interior of the territory.

The Saint Anne's Mission was well linked to other parts of the island via the Royal Road or the *Grand Chemin* (the French term for "highway"). This highway connected the mission to St. Joseph (the administrative centre and capital), the communities dwelling in the north, and the other Catholic missions in the south of Trinidad. The French map (*Map Section 3*) cited above, shows the highway passing right through the *Savaneta Village Indien*. It is very likely that the Royal Road consisted of parts, if not all, of old Indian trails traversing the island of Trinidad, and that the present-day Indian Trail Village Road in Couva was possibly a section of the Royal Road. Mission Road in Preysal Village, previously referred to, was apparently part of the Royal Road (*Grand Chemin*). Note also, the direction of and the bend in the road at the *Savaneta Indian Village and the Saveneta Village Indien* are roughly similar to the ones on Crame's map.

(Often, historians and writers mistakenly claim the modern Savonetta Village as the site of the Catholic mission. Based on the Crame *Sabaneta* Mission's site and the other aforementioned maps' locations of the early Indian village in the eastern region of Couva as well as on historical information, today's Savonetta Village, which is situated in the southwest region of the Couva, where the land is flat, low and near to Savaneta Point on Couva's coast, was apparently not the location of the Catholic mission. Cartographers place the mission several miles inland from the coast, thereby eliminating modern Savonetta Village. Aside from the cartographers' inland placement of the mission, the Capuchin monks planted their mission on the bank of a river where the water was clear. Clear water is found upland, closer to the source of the Saveneta River, which drains the Montserrat Hills. This feature of the river supports the notion that the Savaneta mission was located near the Milton/Indian Trail region, which as indicated before, is at the base of the Montserrat Hills. Besides, the Savaneta River does not flow through the present-day Savonetta Village, which may have been named after Savaneta Point or its savannah terrain.

If the monks were referring to the Savaneta River as a river in the Savaneta region, then the Couva River also fits that description. Like the Savaneta River, referred to above, it drains the Montserrat Hills. Again, clearer water is found upland, closer to its source. This river flows westward, except where it twists and turns in other directions, and empties into the Gulf of Paria, as noted earlier. By the time the Couva River reaches the low lands of Couva, it picks up sediment and other organic materials causing the water to be more opaque and muddier. Finally, the Couva River, does not flow through present day Savonetta Village, and so, once again, disqualifying it as the site of the Savaneta mission.)

[Note: The Couva River is navigable, which made transportation to and from the Amerindian community easier. It is quite plausible that Amerindians travelled by canoe down river to the Gulf or upriver until they encountered higher elevations.]

Map Section 1

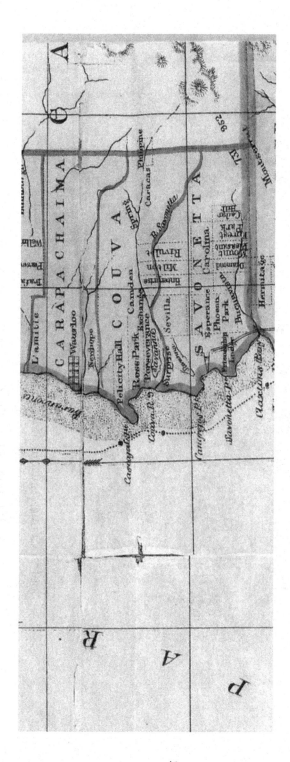

Rivulet and Exchange Sugar Estates and Couva and Savanetta Rivers shown on map. (Section taken from Geological Survey of Wall & Sawkins, London, circa 1860 map in Daniel Hart's *Trinidad and the other West India Islands and colonies*, 1862, 2nd ed.)

Map Section 1A

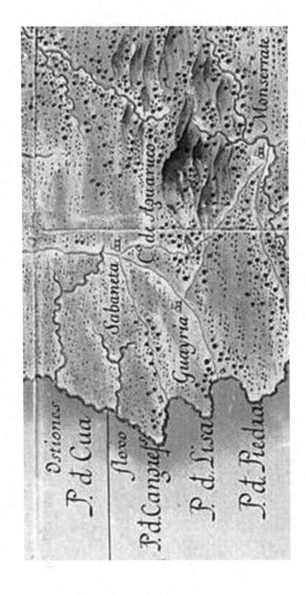

Source: Crame, Agustin. *Mapa de la ysla de Trinidad* by Agustin, 1777.

SPAIN. MINISTRY OF CULTURE AND SPORTS,
General Archive of the Indies, ES.41091.AGI//MP-VENEZUELA,185

Map Section 1B

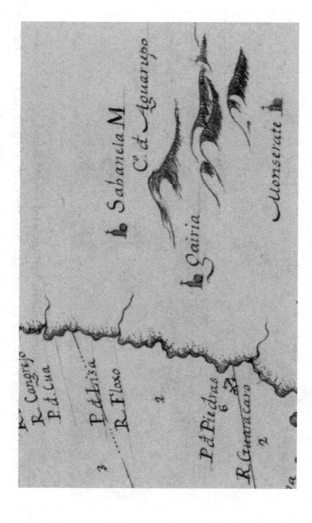

(Section taken from Map showing Trinidad Island and adjacent coast of Venezuela, circa 1700s.
Geography and Map Division, Library of Congress.)
Public Domain

47

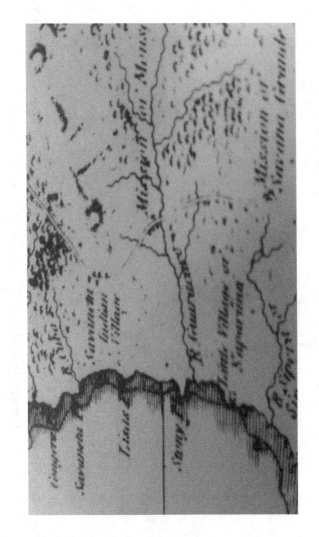

Saveneta Indian Village and Royal Road.

(Section taken from *Plan of the Isle of Trinidad with the Gulf of Paria and the adjacent lands,* W. Faden, Geographer to the King and to HRH the Prince of Wales, Charing Cross, 1ˢᵗ March 1802. From the Lionel Pincus & Princess Firyal Map Division, The New York Public Library.)

Map Section 3

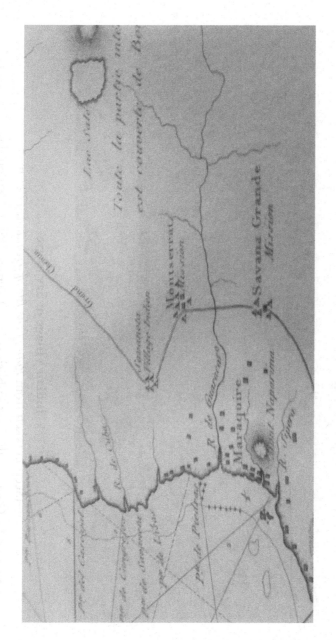

Savaneta Village Indien and Grand Chemin.

(Section taken from *Carte de L'ile de La Trinite*, Publiee au Depot General de la Marine, Paris, **circa** 1804. From the Lionel Pincus & Princess Firyal Map Division, The New York Public Library.)

Map Section 4

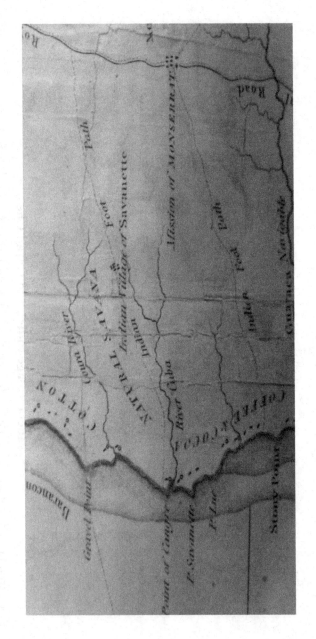

Indian Village of Savanette.

(Section taken from *Plan of the Isle of Trinidad*, 1797 map.
Engraved by George Allen and Published 21ST December 1800, London. From the Lionel
Pincus & Princess Firyal Map Division, The New York Public Library.)

Not long after the selection of the site, the monks built a small 30 feet by 15 feet church and a two-room house for the clergy. The Spanish government provided materials towards the building of the Trinidad missions. As was the custom, the missionary party left behind two of their members, the Reverend Father Felix de Mosset and a young Catalan, to administer the mission before proceeding to Montserrat. It was on Sunday, 23 November 1687 that the church held its first Mass in marking the St. Clement's feast day celebrations (*refer to Text Box*) (Borde, 1876/1982 p. 46).

The Capuchin fathers were church planters who sought to spread the Gospel of Christ to these Amerindians who lived in a remote area, and they did so at great personal hardship, sacrifice, and risks, as will be evident later. Unlike Governor Antonio de Berrio who enslaved the bodies of the natives, the Capuchin fathers sought to liberate their souls by teaching them about the freedom that they had in Christ.

LAYOUT OF THE MISSION

When constructing their missions, the Capuchin monks created layouts similar to the Spanish *pueblos*. Nineteenth century historian, Pierre Gustave Louis Borde, (1876/1982) observed the same pattern and design style in every mission that was established across Trinidad. In the middle of the mission was a square. Majestically dominating the eastern side of the mission was a church adorned with a cross. The other three sides of the square were surrounded by the Amerindian huts. Finally, there were roads bordering the mission (pp. 52-53). The Saint Anne's Mission would therefore have been based on this same pattern, except probably the shape and structure of the huts (See *Drawing 1* by Leeping).

In describing the mission's huts, Borde (1876/1982) states:

These thatched huts were built of posts of hard wood which were put into the ground without being squared or even rough-hewn. They were generally open to all the winds except beneath their pointed roof which was covered by palm leaves, timite or carat which

51

formed the attic which could serve as a bedroom in case of sickness. (pp. 52-53)

Notwithstanding Borde's uniform description of the mission's huts, based on the French map (**circa** 1804) (*see Map section 3*) the huts are seemingly shown as tall and large bell-shaped houses.

The same French map shows a rough visualisation of the layout of the Montserrat mission. The cartographer indicated a square shape in the middle and a rectangular shape east of the square. Large Amerindian bell-shaped huts are located on the other three sides of the square, that is, north, west, and south. The square shape on the map could quite possibly have been the public square found in the typical layout of a mission and the rectangular shape could have been the mission church. Otherwise, the square representation could have been the church (which was usually on the east side) and the

> ### About the St. Anne's Mission Location and More
>
> "On the left bank of the small river Savaneta, they found a convenient spot where they erected a small church, ten *varas* [30 ft.] long and five *varas* [15 ft.] wide, which they dedicated to St. Anne. At its side they also constructed a small presbytery consisting of two little rooms, where they left the Rev. Fr. Felix de Mosset and the young Catalan. It was on the 23rd November, the feast day of St. Clement, that the first Mass was celebrated in this mission."- Borde

rectangle could have been a *cacique's* house, which was larger than the rest of the village's houses and rectangular in shape, or it could have been a community building such as the mission's *cabildo*. The layout of the Saint Anne's would have been similar to that of the Montserrat Mission. In 1714, the Saint Anne's Mission owned a *cabildo* house, which was used for community meetings.

Drawing 1

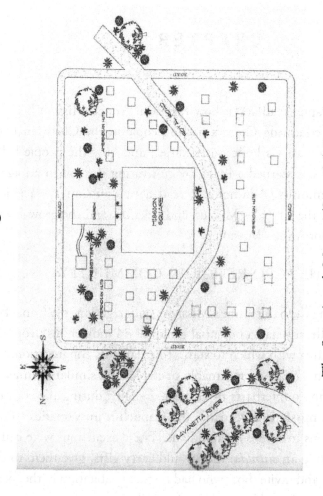

The Saint Anne's Mission (Savaneta) Layout.
Author's Visualisation, largely based on Borde's description of missions
& Map Section 3.
Drawing by Xavier Leeping.

CHAPTER 8

In this chapter read about how the Saint Anne's Mission became the centre of educating Couva's native people in the Christian faith by devoted Roman Catholic missionaries, and how the people led a "civilised life" and earned a living by cultivating the soil in an agro-religious community. Additionally, read about missionary sacrifice, martyrdom at the Arenales Mission and eviction, and the growth and end of the Saint Anne's Mission.

THE AGRO-RELIGIOUS COMMUNITY

In building the Saint Anne's Mission's congregation, the Capuchin missionaries already had a potential group of 34 indigenous people in the Savaneta area with which to start. To enlarge its congregation, the missionaries in Trinidad presumably operated in a similar manner as their Capuchin counterparts in Guiana. Usually, during the start-up period of the missions in Guiana, the Capuchin missionaries would make excursions to secure Amerindians. These excursions were called *entradas*. During an *entrada*, they would carry gifts, give them to the Amerindians, and invite those who had no fixed habitation in the forest to join their mission. Those who voluntarily accepted the invitation followed them to the mission. Nevertheless, it may have taken more than one invitation before the Amerindians were convinced to accept and follow the missionaries to the mission. Others who did not were gently coerced to do so (Strickland, 1896, p. xv; Watters, 1937, p. 143).

Later, there might have been some family transfers from other missions that became operational.

The Saint Anne's Mission functioned as a self-governing frontier institution. The mission took the form of an agro-religious commune, with both secular and religious matters being initially administered by the monks themselves. The monks were responsible for running the daily affairs of the mission, which covered matters of law and order, management, and finance. They were assisted by Amerindians in areas such as administration and policing and in defence of the mission from outside attackers.

The Amerindians who came under the absolute control of the Capuchin monks were congregated at the Saint Anne's Mission and they were educated about religious and secular matters. All the education that the natives received in the missions was not only to save their souls, but also was geared to prepare them for civil life. To communicate with their congregation, the missionaries either used Amerindian translators or learned the native language. Once the Amerindians joined the mission, they were subject to the missionaries for a period of 10 years (Ottley, 1971, p. 26).

Life in the mission entailed worship, education, and work. A key concern of the missionaries was the spiritual welfare of the indigenous people (Strickland, 1896, p. XXII). The Amerindians were taught about the Roman Catholic faith and then baptised. Once baptised, they were obligated to attend Mass on Sundays and on holidays, daily prayers during mornings and evenings, and one or two sessions of religious teaching weekly (de Verteuil, 1995, p. 57). Usually in the Spaniard missions, the Amerindians also learned to speak and sometimes read Spanish and received basic citizenship training. Such would have certainly occurred in the Trinidad missions.

The natives earned a living by cultivating the soil in the mission (Strickland, 1896, Ch. 3, p. XXII). The Amerindians worked two days of the week mandatorily on the mission's communal lands; four other days were allowed as off days for them to look after their own gardens. In return for their labour and their production of food for the mission as well as their conversion to Christianity, they were compensated with free boarding, protection, and exemption from payment of tribute to the Crown. The economic system existing in the mission was communal oriented.

As was the norm, the Trinidad missions were intended to be self-sufficient, and the inhabitants produced food crops for domestic consumption such as cassava, tobacco, maize, plantains and rice crops. Cocoa and surplus rice were produced for export. Notwithstanding the intention of self-sufficiency, the missionaries received an annual allowance from the Spanish government up to 1696.

In order to get an insight into some aspects of life of the Amerindians in the Saint Anne's Mission, one just needs to look at archaeological findings from the nearby Montserrat Mission in Tortuga/Mayo. Life was similar at both. At Montserrat, they hunted peccaries and armadillos, monkeys, and agoutis. They caught sea turtles and also fish that was dried and preserved. They collected molluscs—clams, oysters, conchs, and snails (Boomert, Faber-Morse & Rouse, 2013, pp. 130-131).

Like the typical mission, Saint Anne's was not only engaged in agriculture, as mentioned, but would also have taken to hunting and fishing as their primary activities. The residents would have cultivated most of the same crops (i.e., cassava, corn, plantains, bananas, and tobacco) as well as possibly other crops. The commune also would have grown cocoa as its principal cash crop for export. The revenue generated from cocoa sales would be used for the mission's upkeep expenses—buying tools, furniture, utensils, implements, and supplies. The mission would not have escaped the woes of the devastation that had visited the cocoa sector, as we will see later. Additionally, they would have undertaken the care of farm animals and poultry. They would have also made pottery of the Mayoid series.

The mission system made a major contribution to the economic welfare of the island and to the development of old, remote Couva. It also served to prevent the encroachment of foreign powers into those areas occupied by the missions. Finally, the missions were not just Christianising agencies; as indicated before, they also served as a means for the Spanish Crown to control the Amerindian population after the missions were secularised.

Nonetheless, the mission system did contain some negative aspects, as follows:

- the conversion of the Amerindians was coercive;
- the Amerindians were segregated and isolated from the rest of society once they joined the mission;
- the natives suffered a loss of their cultural traditions as they became Hispanicised;
- the indigenes were not permitted to practice their traditional religious beliefs in the mission and those who were caught doing so were punished;
- the punishment doled out to the Amerindians for the transgression of mission rules was harsh; and
- as will be evident later, the cocoa planters scandalously exploited the missions' Amerindians as labourers.

MISSIONARY SACRIFICE, MARTYRDOM AND EVICTION

The missionaries had to make a huge sacrifice in order to bring the Gospel to the natives of Trinidad. Some missionaries were martyred and others were grievously wounded at the hands of some violent Amerindians. Several others succumbed to natural deaths while soldiering on tirelessly. They toiled at the peril of their lives and endured various hardships such as the unbearable hot weather, disease and health challenges. One of the Capuchin monks who unfortunately died at the hands of the Amerindians was Father Felix de Mosset, the first monk to be assigned to the Saint Anne's Mission. He was killed in 1699 in Trinidad (United States of Venezuela, 1898, p. 268).

In 1699, a shocking rebellion broke out in San Francisco de los Arenales Mission, the fifth mission that had been established by the Capuchin monks on the banks of the Arena River, southeast of San Rafael. The rebels massacred the mission's priests, Friar Estaban de San Feliu, and Friar Marcos de Vichi, and its layman Raimundo de Figuerola. They then celebrated by dancing and shouting and destroyed the mission's small church and its presbytery. Next, they misused the church vestments as loincloths and drank wine from its chalice in a mocking imitation of the Mass. They continued their sacrilegious act by seizing the sacred images of Child Jesus, the Blessed Virgin and Saint Francis and carried them to the mission square where they were smashed. The Spanish Governor, José de León y Echales, was assassinated and most of the members of his official party, including Father Juan Masasieu de Sotomayor (Doctrinaire of Arauca and Tacarigua *encomiendas*), were also killed, while they were all en route to visit the mission. The rebels fled to the eastern coast of the island, and the Spanish authorities, with the assistance of some Amerindians, pursued them. Their rebel leader was killed during the Spanish authorities' battle against the escapees. Others opted to drown themselves in a nearby lagoon. Still others were captured and taken to St. Joseph where they were tried and hanged, and the women and children were made slaves.

Two Amerindian rebel spies of Arenales escaped to Savaneta's Saint Anne's Mission with news of the rebellion. One Captain Calixto, who was attached to the Saint Anne's Mission, arrested them and turned them over to the Spanish authorities. The cause of the rebellion was ascribed to the Amerindians' fear of being severely punished by the Governor if he found them practising witchcraft. These Arenales Amerindian residents had heard that some Amerindians of three other missions— Guayria, Savanna Grande, and Savaneta—had been punished for still practising sorcery when the Governor and his entourage had paid a recent visit to those missions. After the horrific rebellion, the Arena Mission was abandoned.

It was difficult to replace missionaries who were martyred, as there was a scarcity of replacements. This shortage made their work even harder. Despite the great sacrifice, risks and hardships, the Capuchin monks were able to successfully convert many Amerindians to the Roman Catholic faith. Historic reports laud the monks' efforts and reveal that by the year 1707 only a few Amerindians were left to be converted (Padron, 2012, p. 168). The seeds of evangelism planted by the Capuchins in the island's rich soil had produced a bountiful harvest.

In the early 18th century, the monks and the supportive Spanish government encountered a rift over the issue of Amerindian labour.

Cocoa by then had become a lucrative industry in Trinidad that brought prosperity to the island, as stated before, and gave rise to the demands for additional labour (Hollis, 1941, p. 67). The mission system had protected the Amerindians from the avarice of the Spaniard planters and had prevented the disintegration of the indigenous family and other abuses that had been occurring under the *encomienda* system. The Spaniard planters, the worst enemy of the missions, sought their destruction in Trinidad (Watters, 1937, p. 142). They craved the use of the Amerindians in the missions as labourers in their fields and they were granted permission to use them in limited service. The Amerindians were supposed to receive food, wages, and teachings of the Roman Catholic faith in return.

Sadly, the Spaniard planters were quick to renege on their promises and mindlessly exploited the Amerindians. Historian Alfred Claud Hollis (1941) described the situation, saying "The planters, however, disregarded their obligations, and after periods of six or eight months the Indians returned to the Missions exhausted, sick with hunger, untaught, unpaid and unclad." (p. 68)

Discontented with the planters' exploitation and mistreatment of the Amerindians, the employment arrangement was called off by the monks. This led to a serious conflict between the two parties. Don Felipe de Artieda, the Spanish Governor, sided with the powerful planters and called for the removal of monks from the island.

The King of Spain was in favour of the Capuchin monks leaving the island. Consequently, he expelled them in 1708 by a royal order. The king ordered them to work on the mainland; instead, in disobedience, they secretly boarded a contraband-trading vessel and sailed back to Spain (Ottley, 1971, p. 37). Their work had come to an end in Trinidad. It was a severe blow to their missionary endeavour. The Spanish government ordered that secular priests be put in charge of all the Trinidad missions (Watters, 1937, p. 142). The secular priests were responsible for overseeing the religious affairs, while *Corregidores* (i.e., magistrates) were appointed to take care of the judicial, administrative, and labour-related matters. After the missionaries left the island, the Amerindians were made available as labourers for the planters. But the

Amerindians, who were decidedly not happy with this arrangement, began to desert the missions.

In the Spanish colony of Venezuela —and presumably in Trinidad— the position of *Corregidor* was important, but not lucrative. The Viceroy made the appointments to the office, or, as in the case of Trinidad, the Governor apparently. *Corregidores* were Spaniard men who were prominent proprietors in a colony. The office of *Corregidor* combined the duties and responsibilities of a mayor and a justice of the peace (Dauxion Lavaysse, 1813/1820, p. 412).

THE GROWTH AND END OF THE SAINT ANNE'S MISSION

The Saint Anne's Mission continued for over a century. It was reported that in 1764, the mission church and village structures for the most part were destroyed by a fire, which started when the Amerindians attempted to burn the overgrowth that occupied the grounds. The inhabitants were only able to save some religious items from the church, such as a chalice, a holy figure, and sacred vestments. Due to the fire, some of the inhabitants were transferred to the Montserrat Mission. The Spanish government budgeted 300 *pesos* (the peso was the basic unit of Spanish money used in the colonies) for the construction of a new church (Padron, 2012, pp. 171-172; Boomert, 2016, p. 142). As a result, the church was rebuilt by 1785 (Boomert, 2016, p. 144).

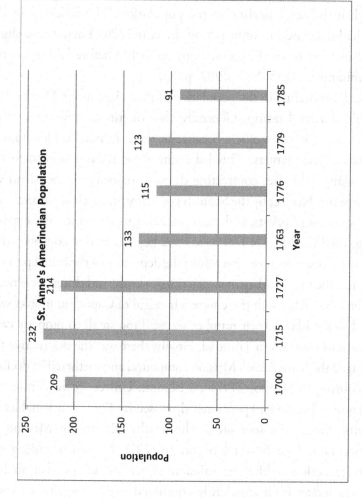

Graph 1

St. Anne's Amerindian Population

Source: Data from Soler, p. 85.

61

Graph 1 provides a picture of the Saint Anne's population during various years. Initially the population rose, but then declined during its latter years. The number of inhabitants in the mission increased from an impressive 209 in 1700 to a new high of 232 inhabitants in 1715. There was a small decline in 1727 when the number was 214. Even with the devastation caused by the fire, part of the mission village survived, although it did see a decline in the population. The residents of the village had decreased to only 115 by the year 1776. There was a slight increase in 1779 when the count came up to 123 before falling to only 91 inhabitants in 1785 (Soler,1982, p. 85).

The sharp decline in the population of the Saint Anne's Mission was the result of several factors. Generally, the Amerindians were deserting the missions in large numbers because of the continued exploitation at the hands of the planters. This led many Amerindians to head to the forests. Many died after contracting diseases imported to the island via the Europeans. Neglect by the Spanish government, a lack of pastoral care due to a shortage of priests, and the secular clergy's ignorance of the native language (Felices, 2003, p. 114) were other key factors that contributed to the missions' disintegration. Ever since the departure of the initial party of Capuchins, the missions began to deteriorate slowly, and things were never again the same. Although there were a handful of Capuchin monks who returned to the island, their number was still too small to properly cater to the various missions in Trinidad. Finally, there was the destructive fire that ravaged the Saint Anne's Mission compound and furthered its decline.

According to Newson (1976), a London University academic, the Saint Anne's Mission had permanently closed by 1794. The inhabitants still living there were sent off to the nearby Montserrat Mission by Governor Don Jose Maria Chacon (p. 221). Notwithstanding the Governor's action, while the mission as an official institution had closed, the *village* itself apparently continued to exist at least for some time ((the French map (circa 1804) shows its existence as an Amerindian *village*, rather than a mission, and, as indicated earlier, labelled *Savaneta Village Indien*. Placing it on the map seems to indicate a functioning Village)). Soon after, this *village* presented itself as a prime location for a sugarcane plantation.

CHAPTER 9

Read this chapter to know about the Spanish King's *Cedula of Population* (1783) that encouraged immigrants to come to Trinidad. Many immigrants (i.e., "cedulants") came to Trinidad from French-speaking Caribbean islands. Learn about the 1783 Royal *Cedula's* success in populating Trinidad, its effect on the economy, and how concomitant geo-politics contributed to immigration to the island. But, the Royal *Cedula* encouraged Black slavery, which changed the demographic makeup of the island.

THE ROYAL *CEDULA* OF 1783: AN INVITATION TO FOREIGN COLONISTS

The next foreigners to arrive on the island of Trinidad were French Catholic Caribbean planters together with their Black slaves, and a small number of Irish immigrants. The year 1766 brought widespread property destruction by a strong earthquake, and the island's star crop—cocoa—underwent complete failure in the year 1772 due to drought conditions (Padron, 2012, p. 171; Carmichael, 1961, p. 35). The feeble progress of the island over the years, combined with these upsetting events, left Trinidad in abysmal condition.

The economy had taken a devastating hit, and the small population was burdened with the aftermath of the economic downfall. The Trinidad government was facing deplorable fiscal problems. The island had always been unable to attract and retain Spaniard settlers.

Just a small number of Spaniard inhabitants remained on the island. Meanwhile, Spain had been making far-reaching reforms both at home and in its colonial possessions during the 1700s. In the Americas the implementation of these reforms, nonetheless, had been slow.

The brief British capture of Havana, Cuba—the island being one of Spain's crown jewels —in 1762 during the Seven Years' War came as a shock to the Spanish Crown. It had to cede Florida to Britain in order to regain Havana by the Treaty of Paris (1763). Spain's King Charles III was determined not to suffer the loss of any more of his colonial possessions. The incident underscored the urgent need for Spain to hasten the pace of sweeping reform, particularly militarily, in its colonies in the Americas. These Bourbon reforms, as they were called, included trade liberalization, commercial, economic, military, and administrative reforms and were aimed, among other objectives, at Spain reasserting control over its colonies in the Americas, increasing royal revenues, stimulating colonial economies and increasing their populations, strengthening the royal government, and reinforcing colonial military defences. Now, Spain rediscovered its long-forgotten backwater island of Trinidad, which once again came within the scope of the Spanish Crown. At that time, Trinidad had been poorly fortified and its economy was in a moribund state. As a result, King Charles III made reforms in Trinidad an imperative in the hope of securing it as a Spanish possession. Trinidad had been part of Spain's defensive chain of posts in the Caribbean from Florida and extending to the northern part of the South American continent (Chinea, 2007, p. 2).

Spain made development of Trinidad's economy and the boosting of its population a priority. Meanwhile, about 1757, the cocoa crop was slowly making a revival, and in order to enhance its commercial progress, in 1765 Spain permitted the island to "freely trade" with other countries within the Spanish Empire, but the concession provoked little response from the settlers (Bottcher, 2007 p. 161; Hollis, 9141, p. 78). In 1776, King Charles III appointed Manuel Falaquez as Trinidad's new governor with instructions to increase the island's population. The island's fertile soil was determined to be suitable for the cultivation of plantation crops, and it became evident that White colonists, capital and slave labourers were needed to populate and economically develop Trinidad. Effectively, a "big push" was needed.

Spain's King Charles III issued a series of decrees to make it easy and attractive for Spanish and foreign Catholics to migrate to Trinidad. It was the first time foreigners were allowed to settle in the Spanish dominion by the lifting of immigration prohibitions, and Trinidad, considered militarily vulnerable and among the least profitable in the Spanish Antilles, became a testing ground for foreign colonisation in Spain's colonies in the Americas (Chinea, 2007, p. 2). The decrees offered land grants and commercial and fiscal incentives lure to settlers. However, these reforms produced only a modest increase in economic production and population growth initially.

A wealthy French Grenadian planter, Philippe-Rose Roume de Saint-Laurent, was one of the immigrants who had been attracted to Trinidad in 1777. He studied the topography, evaluated the resources of the island, and foresaw the latent potential of Trinidad's fertile soils, which offered a golden opportunity, as it was said, for planters to create wealth. He believed that if the Spanish Crown offered enhanced incentives to foreigners, many would come to Trinidad. Saint-Laurent devised an ingenious immigration plan and vigorously promoted it to the *Intendant* of Caracas, Don Joseph de Abalos, who was charged with overseeing Spain's interests in Trinidad, and then to the Spanish court. He internationally marketed Trinidad to immigrants and investors as well. Responding to representations made by the *Intendant* of Caracas, the settled colonists in the island (These would have certainly included Saint-Laurent.), and those foreigners wishing to settle there, King Charles III issued his famous Royal *Cedula* (1783), entitled *Cedula of Population* (Fraser, 1971, Appendix, pp. i - v).

The 1783 Royal *Cedula of Population* was a more complete set of regulations pertaining to Trinidad's foreign settlers, who have been referred to as *"cedulants"*. The *cedula* offered, among other things, generous incentives designed to encourage certain foreigners friendly to Spain to settle in Trinidad in order to develop the island's economy and to grow its population. The decree provided land grants and fiscal incentives (i.e., concessions on certain taxes, payments, and duties) under various articles in order to entice the targeted foreigners to migrate to the island. In effect, the 1783 Royal *Cedula* was a development-by-invitation initiative.

However, on paper the articles of the 1783 Royal *Cedula* were discriminatory in nature. First, Article 1 required a religious test for immigration: foreign settlers had to be Roman Catholic. It was the policy of Roman Catholic Spain to maintain the religious homogeneity of the island. Second, White immigrants of either gender were offered twice as much land as free Blacks and mulattoes. On the one hand, under Article 3, each White immigrant was to be awarded a free grant of 32 acres of land plus 16 acres for every slave he/she owned. On the other hand, under Article 4, each free Black and mulatto immigrant of either gender was to be offered 16 acres of land plus 8 acres for each slave he/she owned. It goes without saying that in principle every creed and race did not find an equal place. Today, the *cedula's* unequal treatment of settlers based on creed and race would be inconsistent with the promise of equality in Trinidad's national anthem.

Cedulants who migrated to the island were required to swear fealty and submit to the laws of Trinidad under Article 2. Only upon taking the oath of allegiance, were they granted land gratuitously forever. Under Article 5, these immigrants were eligible for naturalisation after five years of residence. After becoming citizens of the island, they would be eligible to hold all honourable public service employment and to positions in its militia.

The 1783 Royal *Cedula* received an immediate positive response from the targeted immigrants. It lured some wealthy French—and Irish Catholic—*entrepreneurs* to migrate to the island, bringing their expertise, thousands of Black slaves, and investments along with them from French-speaking Caribbean islands. The *cedulants'* life, slave property and capital all found safety in Trinidad.

The generous offers of the 1783 Royal *Cedula* and the fertile soils of Trinidad were too tempting for many French planters to avoid especially at a time of agricultural difficulties in the French Caribbean islands, such as soil exhaustion and ants' plagues. Others fled after the British seized French-owned islands. Immigration to Trinidad was hastened as planters and their slaves as well as other refugees were forced to flee to the island in order to escape the French Revolution, which spread to the French Caribbean colonies in 1789. Finally, many Haitian immigrants decamped to Trinidad due to a violent slave rebellion in their country.

Catholic immigrants of different political persuasions, races, colours, and classes, free or slave, came from the islands of Martinique, Guadeloupe, St. Vincent, St. Lucia, Grenada, Dominica, and, of course, Hispaniola (i.e., Haiti, as stated before). Even some nobles migrated from France. According to historian Donald Wood (1986), "Royalists and revolutionaries, aristocrats and petit blancs, those who believed in liberty and the rights of man, and those who wanted the old order to continue unchanged, freemen of colour all came to Trinidad and with them came their black slaves." (p. 32)

Trinidad was a start-up nation, offering foreigners an opportunity to prosper. The immigrant planters who met the 1783 Royal *Cedula's* requirements were granted land upon their asking for it in order to cultivate coffee, cocoa, cotton, and sugarcane. Many planters, who took up the offer to migrate and received land grants, put these lands into productive cultivation and made fortunes.

Indeed, Trinidad was a rewarding destination for migrants.

THE 1783 ROYAL *CEDULA'S* SUCCESS

The Royal *Cedula* of 1783 had provided the impetus for the socio-economic growth and development of Trinidad in the latter part of the 18th century and beyond. Expectedly, the Spanish government's liberal policy had its desired effect on the island's economic production and population.

Linda Newson (1976) aptly summarised the effect of the 1783 Royal *Cedula* on the Trinidad economy by remarking:

> During the latter part of the eighteenth century, the problems of labour shortages and the lack of trade that had characterised the earlier part of the century were resolved by a change in the political attitude of the Crown. Foreigners, who were formerly excluded

from Spanish territories, were welcomed and granted considerable concessions, particularly in the form of land grants. Such concessions succeeded in attracting a large number of immigrants, who came with their slaves and established estates producing commercial crops. The development of agriculture, with the trading concessions simultaneously granted to colonists, encouraged trade and enabled the inhabitants to export their products and to import some vital provisions. (pp. 194-195)

The transformative effect of the 1783 Royal *Cedula* on the Trinidad economy is demonstrated by crop production data. In 1777, the total value of crops was about a mere 3,000 pesos (Newson, 1976, p. 194). In 1795, 12 years after the Royal *Cedula's* economic policy was implemented, the value of crop production skyrocketed to 1,984,400 pesos (Soler, 1988, p. 106).

Most of the produce was exported. In 1795, the value of formal exports climbed to 1,588,000 pesos (Soler, 1988, p. 106), whereas they were minimal before the Royal *Cedula* of 1783. As another measure of the growth in trade, the shipping tonnage increased from about 300 per year prior to 1783 to an estimated tonnage of 8,000 per year in 1795 (Trendell, 1886, p. 284). Trinidad was now trading with many Spanish countries in the Caribbean. This was a significant progress, because due to its low level of economic production previously, it had been unable to take advantage of the trade liberalization offered by the Bourbon reforms. Now, Trinidad was able to participate in earnest in the Spanish colonial international trading system in the Antilles. The island also developed into a major *entrepot* for British traders doing business with South America (Bottcher, 2007, p. 165). In 1795, sugar, the leading export, was valued at 642, 000 pesos, followed by other exports—cotton (522,000 pesos), coffee (310,000 pesos), and cocoa (113, 600 pesos). Indigo was also an export crop, but no data was reported for that year (see Table 1). There were also many small farms producing food for local consumption. In 1795, the value of food production for domestic consumption amounted to 396,400 pesos (Soler, 1988, p. 106). Consumables included cassava, corn, plantains, and an array of miscellaneous tropical produce apparently found growing naturally in the savannas.

Table 1

Value of Exports in Pesos (1795)
(Rounded numbers)

Sugar	Cotton	Coffee	Cocoa	Indigo	Total
642,000	522,000	310,000	113,600	-	1,588,000

Source: Data from Soler, p. 111.

Sugar had been a commercial crop cultivated in Trinidad by the Spaniard settlers on a small scale. But the plantation system (as we have come to know it), which was introduced into Trinidad just a few years after the 1783 Royal *Cedula* was issued, gave a huge boost to sugar production on the island. A prime example often noted by historians is the sugar enterprise that was established in 1787 in Port of Spain by immigrant Picot de La Perouse, a French nobleman. His business venture made him a brilliant fortune (Dauxion Lavaysse, 1813/1820, p. 330), and other colonists emulated his success. Thereafter, the sugar sector experienced explosive growth as planters found it to be a very profitable undertaking on the island.

By 1795, this immigration and economic plan had become a reigning success. Trinidad's agrarian economy was experiencing a golden era around this time (Pardon, 2012, p. 179). Part of the credit for the remarkable success has been attributed to the ingenuity of Philippe-Rose Roume de Saint-Laurent and to the prudence of Governor Chacon, who implemented the Royal *Cedula* after taking office in 1784, as well as to Governor Falaquez, his predecessor, who spearheaded earlier reforms. Chacon was an enlightened Governor who instituted administrative and economic reforms on the island and moved the capital to Port of Spain.

An analysis of the demographic data reveals the immense growth of the population of Trinidad. Whereas in 1783, the total population stood at 2,763, by 1795 it had grown monumentally to 15,279 (Soler, 1988, p. 46).

Obviously, the spectacular population growth can be largely

attributed to the incentives offered by the 1783 Royal *Cedula*, although concomitant geo-politics had also contributed to immigration to the island.

Unfortunately, the material success ascribed to the liberalisation of the economy was achieved by immorally enslaving Africans as workers and importing them in much larger numbers than ever before. Not only were foreign settlers granted additional land for every slave they brought in under Articles 3 and 4 of the 1783 Royal *Cedula*, but also Article 15 encouraged the importation of Black slaves into the island by offering a duty-free allowance for 10 years, starting in 1785.

The incentives to import Black slaves into Trinidad had their desired effect. They boosted the island's Black slave population enormously, leading to changes in its demographic make-up. Whereas in 1783 the population of Black slaves in Trinidad stood at a meagre 310, in 1795, the population of this same group exploded to 8,944 (Soler, 1988, p. 51). Meanwhile, the Amerindian population fell from 2,032 in 1783 to 1,078 in 1795 (Soler, 1988, p. 51). In 1783, free Coloureds and Whites numbered only 331 in total. In 1795, this same combined population group grew to an impressive 5,257 in number. Therefore, Black slaves had become the dominant ethnic group (58.5% of the population), outnumbering Whites and free Coloureds (34.4%) and Amerindians (7.0%).

The success of the 1783 Royal *Cedula* is considerably due to a *laissez-faire* capitalist-oriented economic policy instituted in the island by the Spanish government. Under the new policy, the government opened up island's economy to foreign private investors and *entrepreneurs* and provided an enabling environment comprised of a package of economic incentives and deregulatory actions. The policy certainly produced an economic miracle in Trinidad. Today, such a policy can still be successful—without slave labour.

It is interesting to note that in the past Trinidad was a source of Amerindian slave labourers who were captured and exported to the Spanish island of Hispaniola to develop its mines and agriculture. The slave raids contributed to the depopulation of Trinidad. Now, because of the Royal *Cedula* of 1783, Trinidad ironically became the destination for Haiti's (i.e., the French part of Hispaniola) White planters along with their Black slave labourers who were fleeing rebellion to populate and develop the island's economy.

How times changed!

Instead of Bono, the brute, coming to Trinidad to raid and capture Amerindians and then selling them as slaves, it was now Saint-Laurent, the businessman, travelling to the other islands to sell a colonisation scheme in order to persuade the settlers there to migrate to Trinidad.

Philippe-Rose Roume de Saint-Laurent.
Courtesy of Gerard Besson.

CHAPTER 10

Learn about the prominent proprietor, John Nugent and his sugar estate in Couva. Also, read about other notable people who were given land in Couva, including General Cuyler who was reportedly a Protestant.

COUVA'S LAND GRANTEES

The Couva region received many land grants. The list of proprietors of land granted under the 1783 Royal *Cedula* by the Spanish government in the Couva region is shown in *Table 2* below. The names of the proprietors are either French, Anglo (English) or Celtic (Irish or Scottish), or Spanish. The actual locations of the plots of land in either Cascajal or Savaneta are shown on *Map Section 5*. Most of the plots on this map sections are shown as similar-sized squares and are numbered.

Despite the fact that Article 1 of the 1783 Royal *Cedula* had specified that immigrants had to be of the Roman Catholic faith, due to the liberality of Governor Chacon, some protestant Englishmen were allowed to settle on the island.

One prominent proprietor who was granted land under the Royal *Cedula* of 1783 was John Nugent. Born in England in 1737, he was of Irish descent. Reportedly, Nugent's brother-in-law was Edmund Burke, the famed British orator, Member of Parliament, and statesman, and he (Nugent) had been the surveyor general of the London Customs (Bouchard, 2017, n.p.). Unlike other absentee owners, he migrated to Trinidad in 1786. He applied for a land grant on October 1, 1793 to plant sugarcane in the western Cascajal region of Cuva (Couva) and received approval from Governor Chacon soon thereafter. As a prominent planter, Nugent became an advisor to the island's British Governor (as mentioned later) after it changed hands. He resided in Trinidad until 1802, and returned to England to live, thereby becoming an absentee owner at that time. During his absence, Nugent appointed a planting attorney to manage his sugar estate in Couva. He died in Epsom in 1813 at the age of 76.

An extract of the records kept by the British administration in Trinidad containing details of his application and grant is shown below. The particulars of John Nugent's grant of land in Cuva are shown in second to last entry in the extract.

Extract of Land Granted by the Spanish Government According to Forms N 1 & 2

Source: CO 295/35. National Archives, UK. Reproduced with permission.

The location of Nugent's grant is indicated on *Map Section 5*. His sugar estate was called Ross Park (UCL, n.d., para. 3) and located next to the Perseverance and the Exchange Estates (*see Map Section 1*). Part of Ross Park estate would have been situated in or around today's Union and Orange Valley Villages in Couva.

A notable dignitary to have benefitted from the land grant program was General Cornelius Cuyler of the British forces, a British conqueror who captured neighbouring Tobago in 1793 and the former Commander in Chief in the West Indies. General Cuyler, who was reportedly a Protestant, was allocated 1,920 acres of land in eastern Couva (Savaneta) (Mallet, 1802, p. 15), which likely made him the leading individual landowner in Couva at the time. It appears that he did not actually settle on the island nor cultivate his allotment of land. It is very likely that he sold his large parcel of land.

(Proprietor Farfan was apparently one of the elders of a notable family on the island. Land grantee, *V.* Safon, may have been a French or British nobleman, because Mallet was specific in adding a prefix to the name, apparently signifying *Viscount.*)

Table 2

List of Proprietors of Land, granted by Spanish Government, in the Couva Region, 20 March 1797

Region	Names of Proprietors
Casahal (i.e., Cascajal)	Pillard Diguine Ramsay Henitson Iguius Nugent Waldrop Warner Robertson
Savaneta	Dyckson Codet Jantis Favel Samerson Duchaleau Aluson Farfan V. Safon Cofine General Cuyler, (Commander in Chief, 1920 acres)

Source: Mallet, F., Descriptive Account of the Island of Trinidad, 1802

It should be noted that contrary to Mallet's list of proprietors who were granted land by the Spanish government in the Couva region, as of 20 March 1797, which is shown in *Table 2*, General Cuyler and *some* other proprietors may have received their grants from the British governor instead, after the seizure of Trinidad. It appears that the table heading is a bit misleading.

Proprietors Warner and Codet (aka Cadett) jointly owned Couva's Sevilla Sugar Estate; it was sold to planters Gordon and Montgomerie, in 1803, the year after Trinidad officially became a British colony by treaty, which will be revealed later. The estate consisted of 2 sets of sugar works, with cattle mills; contained 1,051 acres of land which produced 1,200 hogsheads of sugar; and possessed 149 "negroes" (i.e., Black slaves) (see *Sale by Auction Advertisement*).

SALE by AUCTION ADVERTISEMENT, 1803 - DESCRIPTION of the SEVILLA ESTATE

ISLAND of TRINIDADA, the importance of which Island is sufficiently ascertained by the late Treaty of Peace. Valuable ESTATE, to be paid for by Instalments.

By PETER COXE, BURRELL, and FOSTER,

At Lloyd's Coffee-house, as will be mentioned in a future Advertisement,

ALL that very valuable Property, the SEVILLA ESTATE, situate Naparini Quarter, in the Island of Trinidada, recently appertaining to C. J. Warner, and James Cadett, Esqrs. but now vested in George Gordon, and Robert Montgomerie, Esqrs. of St. Croix, containing 1051 acres of the best Sugar Cane Land, with a commodious Dwelling, 3 stories high, and suitable offices; 2 sets of sugar works, with cattle mills, one newly finished, for size and convenience deemed the most complete in the West Indies; the whole equal to the working 1200 hogsheads, which the lower lots of land are capable of producing, independent of the upper lots, which, when put in a proper state of cultivation, will yield an equal quantity. This Estate is remarkably healthy, has brick earth, from which the bricks used in the new works were found, and are equally adapted for setting coppers and stills, lies between two extensive savannahs, abounding in pasturage, and worked and watered by the plentiful river Couva, over which there is a very convenient bridge, and within one mile and a half only of the place of shipping. This Estate, which for years past has yielded sugars of the first quality, is to be paid for by four equal instalments, namely, on the 1st of June annually, extending to June 1806; and possesses 149 negroes, consisting of tradesmen of different kinds, and field negroes, with a sufficient supply of mules and cattle. The whole property to be surrendered on the 1st of June next, under engagement of mutual guarantees, as will be expressed in the Particulars and Conditions of Disposal, which will be ready to be delivered one month preceding the sale, and may be then had at the Bar of Lloyd's Coffee-house, and of Messrs. Peter Coxe, Burrell, and Foster, Throgmorton-street, of whom information may be obtained.

Source: The Times. London. January 18, 1803
Public Domain

General Cornelius Cuyler.

British Commander-in-Chief in the West Indies.
Former Couva landowner.

Map Section 5

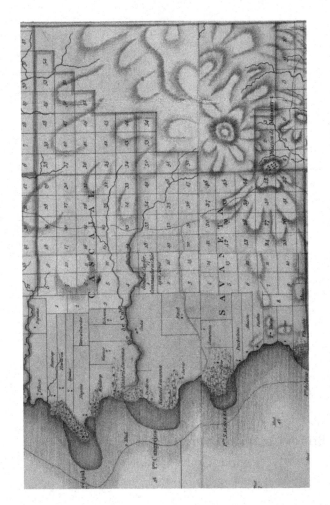

Source: Mallet, F., *A New Map of the Island of Trinidad*, 1802. FO 925/4343.
The National Archives, UK.
Reproduced with permission.

CHAPTER 11

This chapter delves into the impact of the 1783 Royal *Cedula* on the Couva region and how Couva emerged as primarily a sugar plantation economy, which functioned profitably off the brutal exploitation of Black slave labour. Learn about the deplorable conditions of the Black slaves, and just how effective the *Code Noir* (1789) was in protecting them.

THE 1783 ROYAL *CEDULA* AND ITS IMPACT ON COUVA

The Spanish Royal *Cedula* of 1783 had profound socio-economic implications for Couva's evolution. Immigration, land grants, investments, the plantation system, and Black slavery drove economic and social change in the region with lasting effects. Immigrant planters and Black slaves became the newest inhabitants of Couva. They all came to plant crops and to develop Couva's economy.

SUGAR PLANTATION ECONOMY AND BLACK SLAVERY

Sugar became the primary crop that was produced by the planters in Couva. Most of the fertile land of the Couva region granted by the Spanish Government for the cultivation of cocoa, coffee, sugarcane, and cotton was planted with sugarcane—83 percent in Couva/Savaneta and 51 percent in Cascajal (Newson, 1976, pp. 198-199). In the region of Couva, there were 3 rum distilleries and 13 sugar mills in 1802 (Mallet, Appendix).

Couva became an export economy once again, but on a much larger scale, with sugar being its staple export. As a result, Couva grew links to the Spanish Antilles' international markets for sugar. Sugar was sleighed to the Gulf of Paria—sometimes to the mouth of the Couva River—for shipping overseas. It was the beginning stage of sugar developing as Couva's monoculture economy until modern times. As an exporter of sugar, the fortunes of Couva's economy were therefore made dependent on the vagaries of international markets.

The commercial production and exportation of sugar caused Couva to flourish. It didn't take long for the new immigrants to discover the potential of the fertile lands of Couva. Even though Couva has no gold reserves, its soils were a goldmine to the planters. The sugar plantations made the planters rich and politically influential. French political power grew quickly on the island such that in 1786 their representatives held seven of the ten seats in the Cabildo, thereby dominating it.

Couva was introduced to a new economic system based on capitalism and Black slavery—the sugar plantation system. Sugar was grown on plantations, which required large amounts of capital and a large supply of slave labour. In Couva, sugarcane planters now replaced the church planting Capuchin monks and the service of secular priests, and the communal mission life where the inhabitants worked for the common good was taken over by capitalism (which enriched solely the planters), a plantation system, atrocious Black slavery, and even worse exploitation.

The labour-intensive sugar plantations were completely dependent on Black slave labour, thereby making Couva a Black slave economy. Without the Black slaves, the sugar planters would not have been prosperous. Africans had been brought to the French islands in chains and made slaves. Their owners then transported them and their descendants to Trinidad where their slavery condition was perpetuated on the sugar plantation. Additional Black slaves were brought directly from Africa to the island. Black slaves became increasingly important to the planters of Couva, as acquiring more of them meant their obtaining of more land grants. According to historian E. L. Joseph (1838/1970), "It should be observed that the cedula made slaves more important in Trinidad than elsewhere, because it gave their possessors claims for land

in proportion to the number of slaves they possessed or kidnapped...."
(p. 166)

Black slavery was an unspeakably brutal institution. Typically, slaves in the West Indian islands worked under inhumane conditions. Their workdays were long, especially during harvest time. Usually, they toiled all week, except on Sundays and holidays. Their food rations, clothing and shelter, which were supplied by their master or plantation overseer, were meagre. Slaves supplemented their food supply by growing vegetable gardens on their days off. Often, they were sick and went without adequate medical care, thereby succumbing to death. Women were put on work not appropriate for their sex. In many instances, their master or plantation overseer raped them.

Slaves were afforded no human rights whatsoever. Rather, they were considered chattel to be bought and sold. Usually, slaves were exposed to harsh mistreatment at the hands of their unrestrained master or the overseer who, as is well known, generally lacked any sense of humanity and mercy towards his fellow human beings. Unchecked cruel slave owners and overseers invited arbitrary violence against the slaves. Slaves resisted by running away and fought back by rebelling and even in some instances by poisoning their masters. Violence against slaves was used to suppress them and to maintain social order intact as they outnumbered Whites who were haunted by rebellion and poisonings by the slaves (Gibson, 2014, p. 107). The punishment meted out to slaves included severe floggings, mutilations, hangings and other forms of cruelty. Where slave laws existed to alleviate the brutal conditions under which slaves lived, they were more constructed to punish them and to keep them in bondage.

Disintegration of the Black family was one of the key, and most heartless, features of slavery. Disintegration started from the time of their capture from their native tribe in Africa. That meant separation from tribe and family. In cases where family members were abducted, their chances of reuniting with their family were made worse when they were separated and sold to different slave traders, taken to different countries in the Caribbean and elsewhere and again sold to separate planters, and then, sometimes, transferred elsewhere, thereby leaving families scattered. Stable family units that helped and strengthened families were discouraged or disregarded by slave owners (Matthews, 1953, pp. 15-17). Keeping the slave family together was just an incidental matter to the plantation owners. All that mattered to them was a cheap labour supply for the plantation. Whereas under the mission system, the clergy was responsible for the welfare of the Amerindians and had largely protected them from the greedy and abusive planters and the disintegration of the Amerindian family, the sugar plantation system, unfortunately, offered no such protection to Black slaves.

Interestingly, a British observer and Anglican cleric, James Ramsay (1784), who had resided in the West Indies, reported that the planters in the French West Indian colonies tended to reside on their estates and live more in a family way with their slaves than the absentee British planters, and therefore they (the French planters) had a natural affection for them (pp. 53-54).

A few years after the proclamation of the 1783 Royal Cedula, efforts were made to ameliorate the conditions under which the slaves in Trinidad lived and worked. Article 25 of the 1783 Royal *Cedula* had permitted the old and new settlers the right to propose to the Spanish Crown, through the governor, ordinances that were most proper for regulating the treatment of their slaves. Taking advantage of Article 25, the Trinidad planters adopted a set of slave laws based on France's *Code Noir* for its colonies. The new slave code—the *Code Noir* (1789)— proclaimed by Governor Chacon imposed obligations on Trinidad's slave masters regarding the physical and spiritual welfare of the slaves and put limits on the authority of the slave owners for the protection of the slaves.

Under this liberal slave code, the slave owner was required *inter alia* to:

- instruct the slaves in Christianity and to procure them to be baptised and maintain a priest to say Mass;
- provide the slaves with sufficient food, clothing and housing as well as adequate medical care;

- encourage marriages and not prevent slaves from marrying slaves from different plantations;
- not allow slaves to work on holy days;
- not overwork the slaves;
- not compel slaves who were over 60 years old and less than 17 years old to work;
- not give women work unsuitable to their sex;
- not turn adrift old slaves and children to starve;
- not punish any slave with more than 25 lashes for lesser classes of crimes committed and those lashed must be applied in such a manner as not to cause any contusion or effusion of blood;
- leave punishment of the slaves for higher classes of crimes to the law;
- obey the law, otherwise he would be fined and punished, and a judge could even deprive an inhuman master of all his slaves; and finally,
- allow slaves to purchase their freedom (Edwards, 1819, pp. 450-451).

This *Code Noir* (1789) was hailed as the most benign set of slave laws in the Spanish Empire (John, 1988, p. 100), and one English observer, Bryan Edwards (1819), in praising the mildness of the island's slave code, wrote, "Its mildness and equity are honourable to the feelings of the framers of it and of the sovereign by whom it was sanctioned. Nor is there any reason to believe that it was not faithfully executed." (p. 450)

Nonetheless, the *Code Noir* (1789), benign as it was, had its shortcomings. Punishments towards slaves were still kept. Before this slave code was proclaimed, slave mortality rates were high. Compliance with the code would have hopefully lengthened the lives of slaves by improving their welfare. Despite the code's welfare provisions, its benign purpose and the reported French colonial planters' paternalistic relationship towards their slaves, the mortality rates of Trinidad's plantation slaves continued to be high because they were overworked, and suffered from malnutrition, disease, and inadequate medical care. Moreover, they continued to live in poor housing. The code likely had some effect on reducing the burden of the slaves (Newson, 1976, p. 185); however, as it turns out, it did not adequately ease the harsh conditions that the slaves had to endure; only emancipation from slavery, not ameliorating slavery, would end their inhumane burden at last.

Despite being in bondage, Couva's Black slaves found ways to survive and preserve part of their culture.

The bondage and suffering of Blacks in Couva seemed to be perpetual and hopeless. Slavery had been entrenched and profitable. However, the day would come when the twin evil institutions of both the slave trade and slavery would come to an end, as determined British abolitionists would fight to abolish the slave trade and secure the emancipation of the slaves on the island.

Cutting canes, Trinidad by Richard Bridgens, 1836.
Album/Alamy Stock Photo.
Reproduced with permission.

CHAPTER 12

This chapter continues to reveal the impact of the 1783 Royal *Cedula* on Couva. The *Cedula* also brought about a demographic, social and cultural transformation of Couva, from Amerindian to mostly French and African. It sheds light on why the population of Amerindians declined in the coming years. Find out why Trinidad has been a nation of immigrants.

DEMOGRAPHIC, SOCIAL AND CULTURAL REVOLUTION

Immigration under the 1783 Royal *Cedula* brought about a demographic revolution in Couva. The inflow of new immigrants outnumbered the Amerindians, eventually displacing them. Together with the existing Spaniard and Amerindian inhabitants, Couva became a cosmopolitan society.

The official British reports showed the radical demographic transformation of Couva. In 1802, the total population of Couva was reported to be 617, of which there were 35 Whites and 141 Coloured inhabitants; the remaining 441 were Black slaves (Mallet, 1802, Appendix). The Black slaves clearly dominated the demographic composition of Couva, comprising around 71 percent of the total population (*see Graph 2*). Because the entire remaining Amerindian population of the St. Anne's Mission was transferred to the Montserrat Mission, and the census provided a separate category for the Indian missions, the report held no data related to them in

Savenata. Regrettably, the Amerindians were no longer counted as a part of Couva. As indicated earlier, there were seemingly some Amerindians still existing in the *Savaneta Village Indien* after the closure of the Saint Anne's Mission. They would eventually cease to exist in Couva, and they were now a missing part of the town's rich mixture of races and cultures, as someone has commented. Amerindians would soon even stop existing in Montserrat and the immediate surrounding areas.

The Amerindian population suffered a dramatic drop island-wide. Whereas at the start of Spaniard permanent colonisation of the island, Amerindians numbered more than 35,000 in 1593 (according to de Berrio's census), at the end they numbered only 1,082 in 1797 (according to Mallet (1802) (Appendix).

After populating the country for thousands of years, the Amerindians as an ethnic group in Trinidad have become nearly extinct. Only a remnant survives, mostly in the Borough of Arima, located in the northeast part of the island.

Several factors contributed to the group's virtual extinction in the island: aggressive European attacks against the natives, Carib and Spaniard raids for Amerindian slaves, inter-tribal warfare resulting in the Arawaks driving out the Caribs, and the ravages of infectious European diseases, such as smallpox, for which the island's natives had no immunity. The Spaniard raids had thinned out the population. Accounts of visitors in the beginning of the 16th century stated that the island had large numbers of Amerindians. There was also the perception during the better part of the 16th century that Trinidad had a limitless supply of slaves. It is estimated that between 1520 and 1527 some 40,000 members of Trinidad's Amerindian population were taken to Cubagua and Margarita (Glazier, n.d., p. 496). Stephen D. Glazier (n.d.), a former Yale University Research Fellow, opined that "it is possible to estimate Trinidad's population in the 16th century as being anywhere between 15,000 and 250,000 (plus or minus a few Indians)" (p. 496). It was not only the violent Spaniard aggression against natives, slave raids, tribal warfare, and infectious diseases, but also malnutrition due to food shortages and decreased fertility are other factors that caused the decline in the island's population. Still other factors that contributed to the depopulation of the natives were miscegenation and their migration out of the island to other places. In the late 1500s, a large number of Trinidad natives reportedly migrated to the Guianas in South America (Glazier, n.d., p. 497). Displacement from their land was yet another cause of the indigenes leaving the island. Finally, Spaniard planters demanding to put them to work on their plantations may have contributed to their flight.

Many Amerindians words, however, persist in the English language. These include words like hammock, canoe, hurricane, savannah, barbecue, and *cacique* (Thomas, 2003, p. 110), and names of places like Arouca, Chaguanas, Carapichaima and Curepe, to name a few. Today, there is a resurgence of pride in Amerindian heritage and there is public and official recognition of these first people's groups on the island. There are now international policies to promote and protect the rights and dignity of indigenous peoples.

The Amerindian immigrants who migrated to the island serve as a stark reminder that Trinidad has been largely a nation of immigrants. Apart from Africans who were brought in chains as slaves, historically people from various parts of the world have voluntarily immigrated to Trinidad. Some came as political refugees and *entrepreneurs* as the French, others as Asian indentured workers who then settled on the island, and still others as economic migrants from other Caribbean islands, to name a few. In the 1800s, many Spaniard immigrants from neighbouring Venezuela fled to Trinidad owing to war and hardships in their country. Today, people of East Indian, African and Hispanic descent are the newest migrants from South America to Trinidad, albeit most doing so illegally. Once again, Venezuelans, in large numbers, have fled to the island as refugees because of an economic and a political crisis in their country.

The 1783 Royal *Cedula* brought about a change to the island's existing social order. Spanish law established social ordering in the Indies. Through social stratification, the Spanish Crown exerted control of colonial society, and deployed it to ensure obedience to and respect for the monarchy. Social ordering tended to be more rigid. To the extent that social ordering existed in Trinidad society before the issuance of the 1783 Royal *Cedula*, in the top tier were the *Penninsulares* who were the Whites born in Spain and held positions as government and church officials, *encomenderos* and landowners. They were the elites and were considered socially superior. In the next lower tier were the *creoles* that were White and Spaniard, except that they were born of Spaniard parentage in the colonies. They held positions in the church, military and a few sat occasionally in the *Cabildo* (See Newson, 1976, pp. 191-194).

Under the *creoles* were people of mixed Spaniard and Indian races (*mestizos*) or mixed Spaniard and African races (*mulattos and zambos*). These were born *illegitimate*, which contributed to their inferior status. On the one hand, *mestizos* were exempt from forced labour, and laws prevented them from holding positions in the government, church and military. On the other hand, *mulattos* were not exempt from forced labour and suffered the same professional restrictions as the *mestizo*. Later, however, they were allowed to join the army because of their military ability.

Africans were placed in the next lower tier. They were Black slaves and forced to perform the arduous task on plantations. However, their social status ranked higher than that of the Amerindians. They were associated with the Spaniards and, unlike the Amerindians, culturally more akin to them.

Relegated to the very bottom tier of the pyramid were Amerindians. They were poor and conquered people, considered uncivilised and hence socially inferior to the races located in the tiers above them.

After the 1783 Royal *Cedula* was issued, Trinidad's social stratification became less rigid and social mobility improved. Under this royal *cedula*, free Blacks and Coloureds were permitted to be landowners, if eligible for land grants. There was no racial exclusivity for being a landowner. Other factors, too, caused the undermining of the typical plantation social structure based on race.

According to Newson (1976),

> Immigration, together with miscegenation and increasing employment opportunities in the army and trades undermined the racial basis of the social hierarchy, replacing it by one based more on the economic role of the individual in society. Although employment was to a large degree still determined by race, racial divisions, particularly those between the mixed races became less marked and a rise in social status more easily achievable. (p. 193)

The 1783 Royal *Cedula* brought about a transformation of the culture of Couva. As the immigrants from the French speaking islands populated the region, the old Hispano-Indian culture was replaced. Afro-French culture came to dominate Couva. Local developments were shaped by those occurring nationally.

Island-wide societal change was rapidly taking place. A new society was being formed as the old one was vanishing. French power and influence were surging as they grew in population and wealth. As a result, the ascendant French threatened the Spaniards' position on the island. Naturally, tensions arose, and the Spaniards resented the growing dominance of the French.

The French set the tone and style of the society. They influenced the language, dress, food and drinks, architecture, and the arts. Even though Trinidad was Spanish-owned, the island was "colonised" socially and culturally by the French since 1783. French was the language of commerce and society for many years (Ferreria, 2012/2013, p. 68). Effectively, Trinidad had been transformed into a de facto French settlement.

Linguistically, Couva's residents were predominantly French speaking. The enslaved inhabitants spoke French Creole (*Patois*) widely, and the few French residents spoke their mother tongue.

Graph 2

Population of Couva
Year:1802
Total number of inhabitants: 617

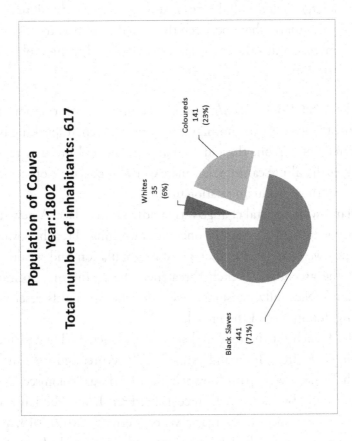

Whites
35
(6%)

Coloureds
141
(23%)

Black Slaves
441
(71%)

Source: Data from Mallet, appendix.

As British colonisation steadily began to take hold on the island after capitulation, as mentioned below, and the British planters increasingly became the dominant sugar plantation proprietors in the region, the English culture and language slowly spread to Couva.

English became the official language of Trinidad in 1814, but Patois naturally persisted for many years thereafter. In fact, households in Couva still commonly spoke Patois. As a result, J. J. Thomas, a one-time schoolmaster in Savaneta, was motivated by his experience of living in the village and his hearing of the Patois language, which was spoken by the villagers, to capture it in a book titled *The Theory and Practice of Creole Grammar*, which was published in 1869 (Vidale, 2005, n.p.).

CHAPTER 13

Learn how the British captured Trinidad and how it put an end to the Spanish rule in the island. A quick recap of all the important events that led to this point and the important people, who played their part in alleviating the tyranny towards the indigenes and in emancipating the Black slaves, are also mentioned in this chapter. Finally, the issue of reparations is touched upon.

THE BRITISH CAPTURE OF TRINIDAD
AND THE END OF SPANISH RULE

In 1796, Spain declared war on Britain, its archrival in the Caribbean. As a result, Spanish-owned Trinidad and its strategic location for entry into Spanish South America became a valuable prize for the British to seize. The island was militarily vulnerable because, despite the promises of the Bourbon reforms, the Spanish Crown had failed to significantly improve Trinidad's defences. That was a costly oversight.

Governor Chacon had been expecting a British attack on the island and requested Spanish reinforcements. A Spanish squadron bound for Cartagena and Havana, commanded by Admiral Apodaca (aka Apodocca or Apocada), was ordered to stop off in Trinidad and to remain there to assist an apprehensive governor militarily. Admiral Apodaca anchored his small squadron, comprising four warships and a frigate, offshore. British naval forces in the Caribbean were ordered to attack Trinidad. On 16 February 1797, a fleet of eighteen British warships under the command of Admiral Henry Harvey arrived in Trinidad's waters, encountering the Spanish naval force. The British had planned to attack the Spanish squadron and land troops in Trinidad the next day. Seeing that his small squadron was outmanned and outgunned by the larger British fleet, Admiral Apodaca chose not to do battle with such an overwhelming force because he and his squadron's captains unanimously agreed that it was futile to do so, and neither could his ships escape. Unexpected by the British, at 2 o' clock in the morning of their planned military operations, Admiral Apodaca resorted to setting four of his five warships on fire in order to prevent them from being captured by the enemy, consequently making the seizure of Trinidad easier. (The remaining ship was captured.)

SELECTED ARTICLES from
ARTICLES of CAPITULATION

Dated 18 February 1797

8. *All the private property of the inhabitants, as well as the Spaniards as such as may have been naturalized, is preserved to them.*

10. *The Spanish officers of administration, who are possessed of landed property in Trinidad, are allowed to remain in the island, they taking the oath of allegiance to his Britannic Majesty; and they are further allowed, should they please, to sell or dispose of their property, and retire elsewhere.*

11. *The free exercise of their religion is allowed to the inhabitants.*

12. *The free-coloured people, who have been acknowledged as such by the laws of Spain, shall be protected in their liberty, persons and property, like other inhabitants....*

15. *All of the inhabitants of Trinidad shall, within thirty days from the days thereof, take the oath of allegiance to his Britannic Majesty, to demean themselves quietly and faithfully to his Government, upon pain, in case of non-compliance, of being sent away from the island.*

———

Source: Joseph, E. L. (1838/1970).
History of Trinidad, pp. 197-198

The Capture of Trinidad, 1797 by Nicholas Pocock.
The Picture Art Collection /Alamy Stock Photo.
Reproduced with permission.

On 17 February 1797, the British, under the command of Sir Ralph Abercromby—the Commander in Chief of British land forces—then invaded Trinidad, and the Spanish Governor Chacon quickly surrendered without putting up much resistance (Carmichael, 1961, pp. 40-41). Abercromby, Harvey, and Chacon signed a capitulation agreement the next day, 18 February 1797, at the town of Port of Spain, Trinidad. Under the terms of capitulation, religious freedom and property rights were recognised, and the inhabitants—as well as Spaniard administrative officers who possessed landed property in the island—were required to pledge allegiance to the Britannic Majesty (Joseph, 1838/1970, pp. 195-198). Abercromby assumed temporary charge as administrator of the newly-captured Caribbean island. He ordered a survey of Trinidad, which resulted in an 1802 official report and map by F. Mallet. Abercromby departed from the island after about two months of the signing of the capitulation, appointing his aide de camp, Lieutenant Colonel Thomas Picton, to the office of British Governor and Commandant of Trinidad. At that time, the island endured a state of disorder, and Picton ruled as a tyrant.

Sir Ralph Abercromby after John Hoppner.
© National Portrait Gallery, London.
Reproduced with permission.

On 25 March 1802, the Treaty of Amiens ceded the sugar-producing colony Trinidad to Britain, making the island a British colony. After three centuries, the Spanish rule of the island had officially ended. However, the British continued with most of the Spanish practices and laws until they felt the need to establish new ones (Carmichael, 161, p. 43).

Significantly, the religious barrier to immigration was removed under the British. Britain held the island until 1962 when it granted Trinidad its independence.

At the time of the formal British takeover of Trinidad, the Saint Anne's *Mission,* which existed in the wilderness of old Couva, had been abolished. Nonetheless, the *village* itself, without mission status, was apparently still in existence, possibly as a living and breathing community, at least for some time, as the *Savaneta Village Indien.* But even this village—and whatever other Amerindian settlements that likely existed in the region—would eventually vanish. The regional landscape had been transformed into sugar plantations mostly. Sugar mills, rum distilleries, planters' houses and slave dwellings within the plantations dotted the region.

CODA: PROTECTORS, JUSTICE, FREEDOM, REPARATIONS, etc.

The history of the Amerindians in Trinidad under Spanish colonial rule is one of pervasive injustice and tyranny. Fortunately, the emergence of protectors attempting to take action on their behalf to deliver them justice and release them from oppression has been a recurring theme of Trinidad's colonial history. Against the treachery and brutality of the Spaniard slavers, the abuses of the *encomenderos* and the virtual slavery of the Amerindians under the *encomienda* system, Las Casas, the *Protector of the Indians,* would arise to expose the brutality against them. He fought for Trinidad's Amerindians, and occasionally the Spanish Crown would benevolently intervene to reform the colonial system with laws and decrees and end the abuses against the Amerindians, although the colonists resisted and some reforms were either postponed, rarely enforced, or ineffective.

The New Laws, though, re-established the fundamental principle that Amerindians were free people.

The tyranny of Antonio de Berrio would be punished by Raleigh, as if he was a *deus ex machina*, who intervened as an agent of the British Queen to liberate the Indian leaders and he promised that she, as a deliverer, would free all of the Indians from Spaniard atrocious tyranny and oppression. The Capuchin clerics would protect the Amerindians from the abuse of the exploitative cocoa planters, until they could no longer do so. The history of the Blacks during Spanish colonial rule is one of slavery, oppression and violence. The *Code Noir* (1789) promulgated by Governor Chacon attempted to ease the harsh treatment of slaves, but it had its flaws. In later years, the White British abolitionists would fight to free the Black slaves and be victorious.

As compensation for the loss if their "property", Trinidad's sugar plantation owners were paid just over £1 m. by the British government.

Today, there are rising calls in the Americas and elsewhere for official apologies and for the payment of reparations to the surviving descendants of both the indigenous peoples and the Black slaves to compensate them for the historical wrongs committed against their ancestors. After satisfying these pre-conditions, then there is expected to be reconciliation between the perpetrators and the victims' descendants.

CHAPTER 14

This chapter sheds light on how key institutions like law and order, religion, and education were established in a reborn Couva. Learn how the following years led to the re-emergence of a Roman Catholic community in Couva, which had been abolished with the closure of the Capuchin Saint Anne's Mission in Savaneta. Read about the formation of the new Exchange Village and how the Trinidad Government Railway was extended to reach this new place. Officials were also appointed to administer the village's governmental services. Learn about the evolution of modern Couva as it is today.

THE RENAISSANCE OF COUVA

In the several decades following the shutting down of the Saint Anne's Mission in the Milton/Indian Trail region, modern Couva was spawned as the Exchange Village, which was located a few miles to the west of the closed Catholic mission.

Couva's Black slaves were emancipated by British law in 1834, as noted earlier, but they had to serve a period of apprenticeship until they were finally free. Apprenticeship ended in 1838. In order to meet the basic needs of a new society that was anticipated to be formed after full emancipation, the Trinidad government and the regional sugar planters in the years immediately following began to establish key institutions— law and order, religion, and education—in Couva. By 1836, a small police station— apparently a wooden structure—was established by the government to maintain law and order, with British Lt. Governor Hill coming to visit it that year.

In 1835, the Commandants, Planters and free Inhabitants of the Couva region and the districts of Chaguanas and Point a Pierre held a public meeting and resolved to establish a Roman Catholic Church and a presbytery. A committee was appointed to implement the resolution. It first raised private funds, mostly donated by planters. In 1836, the committee contracted for the construction of the church that was named Saint Paul's Roman Catholic Church. The committee had purchased part of the building materials. But finding that their efforts would be paralysed without the assistance of the government, the residents petitioned Lt. Governor Hill and, as a result, the government provided public aid for the establishment of this religious institution as well as for payment of a cleric's salary. The new church, which was built of wood in the savannah of Couva, would provide a place of Christian worship for the community, the majority of which were Black apprenticed labourers who had been previously receiving instructions and the blessings of the Roman Catholic faith on the plantations without such a formal facility and resident clergy. The regional residents had also intended, as part of their plan, for the establishment of a school (in the form of an annexed schoolroom) for the moral and other useful instruction of the children of mostly the freed Blacks at all times, and for adults on Sundays and holidays. Consequently, at this time there was a re-emergence of a Roman Catholic community in Couva that had been abolished with the closure of the Saint Anne's Mission in Savaneta. Around the same time, a new Anglican community too was being formed in the new village.

In the years soon after the end of apprenticeship, Couva saw the embryonic formation of the new village of Exchange. Early settlers in the new village, who were, as expected, mostly freed Blacks, acquired plots of land and built houses. To meet the long-distance transportation needs of this growing population centre and for commercial purposes, the Trinidad Government Railway was extended to the newly formed Exchange Village, Couva in 1880. The village community grew up and surrounded the Saint Paul's Roman Catholic Church, the Exchange Roman Catholic School, and the government centre that housed the warden's office (which contained a savings bank), the police station (which housed a courtroom), the Department of Works, the old post office which was established in 1851, the railway station, the station master's house (now demolished), and the water cisterns (now community swimming pools) which stored the village's water supply. Finally, officials were appointed to administer the village's governmental services.

In modern times a separate court building; the old public car park (now replaced); the local governing body, Couva/Tabaquite/Talparo Regional Corporation; Inshan Ali Promenade; Hannah Dixon Children's Playground; and a public library were all added to this cluster.

MODERN COUVA

With years and years of urban development, the small village of Exchange, Couva has now transformed into a town. It has its own dedicated library, district hospital, fire station, three high schools, several churches, modern sporting facilities, and an active airfield. The town is well connected with a comprehensive infrastructure network, proper transportation facilities, water and power services, and modern communication systems. Its high street, that is, the Southern Main Road, which may have once been an Indian footpath, is buzzing with business activities. Present day Couva has emerged as a pulsating, political, commercial, and university centre supporting a fast-expanding population. The town is prosperous and is home to multicultural ethnicities, with English being the solely spoken language.

The sugar plantations, which were once considered a money-minting investment, do not exist anymore, mainly because of their low return prospects. Part of the land, which was once used for sugarcane plantations by state-owned Caroni Limited, is now used for public housing and industrial plants. Separately, the Trinidad and Tobago government distributed a large part of the defunct company's lands to its former workers for private housing and for agricultural development. They are the latest land grantees.

The world-famous Point Lisas Industrial Estate and Port is also located in Couva, and it has transformed the town into the industrial capital of Trinidad. This 2,125-acre industrial estate is bustling with manufacturing activity—predominantly petrochemicals. In both the industrial estate and the Couva region there are several state-owned enterprises along with private companies. The website of the Point Lisas Industrial Port Development Company, which manages the estate and port, boasts of the facility being home to more than 100 companies, with their collective investments valued at over $2 billion USD in 2019 (Point Lisas Industrial Port Development Company (n.d.)·, paras. 1-2). Indeed, Couva has a relatively more successful mixed economy today compared to its neighbouring Venezuela, a failed socialist state.

It is interesting how Couva's economy has evolved over time. First there was the simple traditional economy of the natives in early times, then the purported feudal-like *encomienda* system introduced by Spain, followed by the Saint Anne's Mission communal economy established by Roman Catholic missionaries, which was superseded by *laissez-faire* capitalism promoted by the *Cedula of Population* (1783), where the sugar plantation functioned profitably off the planters' brutal exploitation of Black slave labour and, finally, today a mixed economy—an economic system which combines elements of both capitalism and socialism—embraced by the independent country's successive governments.

Today Couva is a great place to live, work, play, and study, as well as to do business. It is a town that is crackling with energy and infused with dynamism. With all the urban development and economic indicators working in favour of Couva, the town possesses bright prospects for the Trinidad and Tobago government to consider elevating it to borough status.

Couva's Business District, 2013.

Credit: Steve Dixon.

REFERENCES

Basil, R. A. (2009). *Myths and Realities of Caribbean History*. Tuscaloosa: University of Alabama Press

Boomert, A. (2016). *The Indigenous Peoples of Trinidad and Tobago: From the First Settlers until Today*. Leiden: Sidestone Press

Boomert, A., Faber-Morse, B. & Rouse, I. (2013). *The 1946 and 1953 Yale University Excavations in Trinidad*. (No. 92). New Haven: Yale University Department of Anthropology and the Yale Peabody Museum of Natural History

Borde, P. G. L. (1982). *The History of Trinidad under the Spanish Government*. (*Vol. 2*. 1622-1797). (A.S. Mavrogordato, trans.). Port of Spain: Paria Publishing Co. (Original work published 1876)

Bottcher, N. (2007). Neptune's Trident: Trinidad, 1776–1840: From Colonial Backyard to Crown Colony. *Jahrbuch für Geschichte Lateinamerikas*. (*Vol. 44*, Issue 1, 157–186). Retrieved 23 March 2019, from https://doi.org/10.7767/jbla.2007.44.1.157.

Bouchard, B. (n.d.) *The Nugent family from Ireland to Bath & London and, briefly on Clay Hill, Epsom*. Retrieved 18 October 2018, from http://www.epsomandewellhistoryexplorer.org.uk/NugentFamily.html

Campbell, C. C. (1992) *Cedulants and Capitulants: The Politics of the Coloured Opposition in the Slave Society of Trinidad, 1783-1838*. Port of Spain: Paria Publishing Co. Ltd

Carmichael, G. (1961). *The History of the West Indian islands of Trinidad and Tobago, 1498-1900*. London: A. Redman

Carrada, A. (n.d.). *The Dictionary of the Taino Language*. Retrieved 18 December 2018, from http://www.alfredcarrada.org/notes8.html

Chinea, J.L. (2007). Irish Indentured Servants, Papists and Colonists in Spanish Colonial Puerto Rico, ca. 1650-1800. In *Irish Migration Studies in Latin America, Vol. 5, No. 3*, 171-181. Retrieved 11 March 2019, from https://www.academia.edu/24907710/_Irish_Indentured_Servants_Papists_and_Colonists_in_Spanish_Colonial_Puerto_Rico_ca._1650-1800_

Cohen, J. M. (Ed & Trans.). (1969). *The Four Voyages of Christopher Columbus. Being his own log book, letters and dispatches with **connecting** narratives drawn from the Life of The Admiral by his son Hernando Colon and other contemporary historians*. London: Penguin Books

Council of Castile (1510). The Requiremento. (n.p.). Retrieved February 28, from https://nationalhumanitiescenter.org/pds/amerbegin/contact/text7/requirement.pdf

De Armellada. Cesareo. (1960). Por *la Venezuela indigena de ayer y de hoy*. (*Tomo I: Siglos XVII. p.94 y XVIII, Monograph No. 5, Siglo XI*, pp. 93-101.) Caracas: Sociedad de Ciencias Naturales la Salle.

De Barcelona, A. (1687). Viaje desde el Puerto De Cadiz a la Isla de Trinidad y Recorrido de la Misma. *Diary*. Doc. No. 16.

De Barcelona, A. (1687). Viaje Desde El Puerto De Cadiz A La Isla De Trinidad Y Recorrido De La Misma. In P. Fray Cesareo de Armellada. (1960). *Por la Venezuela indigena de ayer y de hoy. (Tomo I: Siglos XVII y XVIII, Monograph No. 5, Siglo XI,* pp. 93-101.) Caracas: Sociedad de Ciencias Naturales la Salle.

De Las Casas, B. (2008). *A Brief Account of the Destruction of the Indies.* BN Publishing. (Original work published1542)

De Verteuil, A. (1995). *Martyrs and Murderers, Trinidad 1699.* Port of Spain: Litho Press

De Verteuil, L.A.A. (1884). *Trinidad: Its Geography, Natural Resources, Administration, Present Condition, and Prospects.* (2nd ed.).London: Cassell and Company, Limited

Dauxion Lavaysse, J.J. (1813/1820). *A statistical, commercial, and political description of Venezuela, Trinidad, Margarita, and Tobago: containing various anecdotes and observations, illustrative of the past and present state of these interesting countries; from the French of M. Lavaysse: with an introduction and explanatory notes, by the editor Edward Blaquiere.* London: G and WB Whittaker

Edwards, B. (1819). *The History, Civil and Commercial, of the British West Indies.* (5th ed.,Vol. 4). London: T. Miller

Felices, F. B. (2003). Catholic Church in the Caribbean. In *New Catholic Enclycopedia.* (Vol. 3, pp. 108- 122). Detroit: Gale

Ferreira, J. S. (2012-2013, October - March) Patois in Trinidad and Tobago: From John Jacob Thomas to Lawrence D. Carrington. *STAN,* 66-71. Retrieved July 30, 2018, from https://sta.uwi.edu/stan/archives/STANoct2012dec2013.pdf

Fraser, L. M. (1971). *History of Trinidad, 1781 to 1813. (Vol. 1).* London: Frank Cass & Co. Ltd. (Original work published 1891)

Gibson, C. (2014). *Empire's Crossroads: A History of the Caribbean from Columbus to the Present Day.* New York: Atlantic Monthly Press.

Glazier, S. D. (1980). Aboriginal Trinidad in the Sixteenth Century. *The Florida Anthropologist, Vol. 33, No 3.* 152-159

Glazier, S. D. (n.d.). *To Have But Not to Hold: Spanish Trinidad From 1498to 1592.* n.p., 494-500. Retrieved 16 January 2019, from http://ufdcimages.uflib.ufl.edu/AA/00/06/19/61/00367/11-45.pdf

Grant, K. J. (1923). *My Missionary Memories,* Halifax: The Imperial Publishing Co., Limited.

Hanson, E.R. (Ed.). (1967). *South from the Spanish Main.* New York: Delacorte Press.

Helps, A. (1856). *The Spanish Conquest in America, and its Relations to the History of Slavery and to the Government of Colonies.* (Vol. II). New York: Harper & Brothers

Hollis, A. C. Sir. (1941). *A Brief History of Trinidad under the Spanish Crown.* Trinidad and Tobago: A.L. Rhodes, M.B.E.

John, M. A. (1988). *The plantation slaves of Trinidad 1783-1816, A mathematical and demographic enquiry.* Cambridge: Cambridge University Press

Joseph, E.L. (1970). *History of Trinidad.* London: Frank Cass & Co. Ltd. (Original work published 1838)

Laurence, K.M. (1975).Continuity and Changes in Trinidadian Toponyms. In *Nieuwe West Indische Gids. Vol. 5* (Issue1). 123- 42. Retrieved 18 October 2017, from http://booksandjournals.brillonline.com/docserver/22134360/50/1/22134360_050_01_s12_text.pdf

Loven, S. (2010). *Origins of the Tainan Culture, West Indies.* Tuscaloosa: The University of Alabama Press. (Original work published 1935)

Mallett, F. (1802). *A Descriptive Account of the Island of Trinidad.* London: Printed for W. Faden

Matthews, B. Dom (1953). *Crisis of the West Indian Family, A Sample Study.* Port of Spain: Government Printing Works

Newson, L. A.(1976). *Aboriginal and Spanish colonial Trinidad: a study in culture contact.* London; New York: Academic Press.

Ottley, C. R. (1971). *Spanish Trinidad: An Account of Life in Trinidad, 1498-1797.* Trinidad: Longman Caribbean.

Padron, F. M. (2012). *Spanish Trinidad.* Kingston: Ian Randle Publishers.

Point Lisas Industrial Port Development Company (n.d.) *Estate management: Overview.* Retrieved 14 January 2019, from http://www.plipdeco.com

Pope Alexander VI. (1493). *Inter caetera*, Encyclopaedia Virginia. Retrieved 11 January 2018, from https://www.encyclopediavirginia.org/Inter_caetera_by_Pope_Alexander_VI_May_4_1493

Raleigh, W. Sir. (1887). *The Discovery of Guiana and The Journal of the Second Voyage thereto.* London, Paris, New York: Cassell & Company, Limited. (Original work published 1596).

Ramsay, James, Rev. (1784). *An Essay on the Treatment and Conversion of African Slaves in the British Colonies.* London: James Phillips

Ray, J. H. (2015). Procurement and Use of Chert from Localized Sources in Trinidad. *Journal of Caribbean Archeaology, 15,* 1-28

Rogozinski, J. (1992). *A Brief History of the Caribbean, From the Arawak and the Carib to the Present.* New York: Meridian

Sales by Auction. Advertisement. (1803, January 18). The Times, p. 4. Retrieved on 22 November 2019, from https://go.gale.com/ps/retrieve. do?tabID=Newspaper

Soler, R. S. (1988). *Inmigracion y Cambio Socio-Econmico en Trinidad (1783 - 1797)*. Sevilla: Escuela de Estudios Hispano-Americanos de Sevilla.

Strickland, Joseph, Rev. (1896). *Documents and Maps on the Boundary Question between Venezuela and British Guayana. From the Capuchin Archives in Rome. With a Brief Summary of the* Question. Rome: Printed by the Unione Cooperativa Editrice

Sued-Badillo, J.(Ed). (2003). *General history of the Caribbean.* (Vol. 1). Autochthonous societies. Oxford: UNESCO Publishing

Tenenbaum, Barbara A. (Ed.). (1999). *Latin America, history and culture: an encyclopedia for students.* (Vol. 4). New York: Charles Scribner's Sons

The Historical Society of Trinidad and Tobago, Publication (n.d.). *A Royal Cedula to the Governor of Trinidad and Guayana.* (Pub. No. 570). (n.p.). Retrieved 22 March 2019, from http://library2.nalis.gov.tt/gsdl/ collect/hist3/index/assoc/HASH017e/a8b3fb94.dir/doc.pdf

The Trinidad Historical Society. (n.d.). *Notarial Record of the Founding of the Town of San Josephe De Oruna. (Extracted 3rd October 1592).* (Pub. No. 15). (n. p.). Retrieved 5 November 2018, from http://ufdc.ufl.edu/ UF00080962/00003

The Trinidad Historical Society (1594). *Decree of the Council of the Indies, ordering Antonio de Berrio to leave Trinidad to Francisco de Vides.* (Pub. No. 19). (n.p). Retrieved 24 March 2019, from http://ufdc.ufl. edu/UF00080962/00007

Thomas, H. (2003). *Rivers of Gold: The Rise of the Spanish Empire, From Columbus to Magellan.* New York: Random House.

Trendell, J.R. A. (Ed.). (1886). *Her Majesty's Colonies. A Series of Original Papers Issued under the Authority of the Royal Commission.* (2nd ed.) London: William Clover and Sons, Limited

UCL. (n.d.). *Ross Park, Trinidad.* Retrieved 24 March 2019, from Legacies of British Slave-ownership database. http://www.ucl.ac.uk/lbs/project/details/

United States of Venezuela. (1898). *Venezuela-British Guiana Boundary Arbitration, The Case of the United States of Venezuela, Before the Tribunal of Arbitration to Convene at Paris Under the Provisions of the Treaty Between the United States of Venezuela and Her Britannic Majesty Signed at Washington February 2, 1897.* (Vol. 1). New York: The Evening Post Job Printing House

Vidale, Akins. (2005). *Biography: John Jacob Thomas.* TriniView. com. Retrieved 30 September 2018 from http://www.triniview.com/TnT/080705.html

Whitehead, N. L. (1984). Carib cannibalism. The historical evidence, *Journal de la Societe des Americanistes, Tome 70,* 69-87

Watters, M. (1933). A History of the Church in Venezuela,1810-1930. Chapel Hill: The University of North Carolina Press

Watters, M. (1937). The Colonial Missions in Venezuela. *The Catholic Historical Review, Vol. 23, No. 2,* 129-152 Retrieved 22 February 2019, from https://www.jstor.org

Williams, W. (1973). *A Description of Trinidad 1881-1882.* (Unpublished manuscript, N.L.W. MS. 17, 267 D. Transcribed Courtesy of the National Library of Wales)

Wood, D. (1986). *Trinidad in Transition: The Years after Slavery,* London: Oxford University Press for Institute of Race Relations

INDEX

118

Printed in the United States
By Bookmasters